On Her Silver Rays

A Guide to the Moon, Myth and Magic

On Her Silver Rays

A Guide to the Moon, Myth and Magic

Frances Billinghurst

MOON
BOOKS
Winchester, UK
Washington, USA

JOHN HUNT PUBLISHING

First published by Moon Books, 2023
Moon Books is an imprint of John Hunt Publishing Ltd., No. 3 East Street, Alresford
Hampshire SO24 9EE, UK
office@jhpbooks.net
www.johnhuntpublishing.com
www.moon-books.net

For distributor details and how to order please visit the 'Ordering' section on our website.

Text copyright: Frances Billinghurst 2022

ISBN: 978 1 80341 149 1
978 1 80341 150 7 (ebook)
Library of Congress Control Number: 2021953156

A CIP catalogue record for this book is available from the British Library.

Design: Matthew Greenfield

UK: Printed and bound by CPI Group (UK) Ltd, Croydon, CR0 4YY
Printed in North America by CPI GPS partners

We operate a distinctive and ethical publishing philosophy in
all areas of our business, from our global network of authors to
production and worldwide distribution.

Contents

To my Lady of the Night Sky
Forever guiding me gently onwards.

Other Books by Frances Billinghurst

Dancing the Sacred Wheel:
A Journey through the Southern Sabbats

In Her Sacred Name:
Writings on the Divine Feminine

Call of the God:
Exploring the Divine Masculine within Modern Paganism
A Wytch's Circle

Encountering the Dark Goddess:
A Journey into the Shadow Realms

A Little Book of Wicca

Contemporary Witchcraft:
Foundational Practices for a Magical Life

Acknowledgement to Country

I acknowledge the Kaurna people of the Adelaide Plains as the traditional custodians of the land upon which this book is written. In doing so, I acknowledge their elders, past, present and emerging, and pay respect to their connection to the land and cultural beliefs.

Acknowledgement to Ancestors

I acknowledge all the ancestors of place and bloodline who have gone before and who have yet to come.

She rises and sets silently, subtly controlling the watery bodies below. The luminous globe who has been the subject of beauty and inspiration for poets and dreamers alike across the ages. Creating a sense of wonder, we stand in awe of her magnificence and shudder when she disappears.

To the moon in all her reflected glory, to all the moon worshippers and those who gather beneath her beams do I dedicate this book.

May she silently guide you to fulfil your dreams.

Pray to the moon when she is round
Luck with you shall then abound
What you seek for shall be found
In seas or sky or solid ground.[1]

"And when the clear moon, with its soothing influences, rises
full in my view ... from the wall-like rocks, out of the damp
underwood, the silvery forms of past ages hover up to me,
and soften the austere pleasure of contemplation."
Goethe's "Faust" (Hayward's translation, London 1855)

Disclaimer

The information given as part of this book is strictly for educational and entertainment purposes. In absolutely no way is it meant as a substitute for proper medical diagnosis and treatment by registered healthcare professionals. It is very strongly recommended that you consult a licensed healthcare practitioner for any physical or psychological ailments you may have.

Introduction

*You have no option but to feel the rhythm of the universe
in the rhythm of your heart.*[2]

The moon fascinates me. I can gaze at her beauty endlessly as
she evolves from the first sliver of hope in the night's sky to the
fertile crescent of the waxing moon, followed by the abundant full
moon before she wanes and eventually disappears altogether,
only to reappear a few days later.

As a reflection of the sun's rays, there is something mysterious
about the moon. She (I usually consider the moon as female
despite the existence of moon gods) offers a calming presence most
of the time. Yet, throughout her cycle, Lady Lunar pulls at our
subconscious and entices us to loosen our restraints. She touches
us on a deep soul level, reminding us of our animalistic and primal
heritage. Have you ever wanted to simply howl at the moon?

Mother Moon, the wise woman, will share her secrets with
us if we take the time to stop and listen, to connect with her
gentle ebbing and flowing. These secrets lie deep within us and
cannot be experienced through someone else's words. Have you
forgotten how to get in touch with them or even how to recognise
them in our frantic modern world? Gaze at the moon for longer
than a casual glance and she will remind you once again.

During her 29½ day cycle, the moon waxes and wanes. Her
mysterious forces exert their influence, not only on our planet
but also on ourselves. For many centuries, humankind has
planted by her pull on Earth, conducted rituals according to
what phase she is in, used her light as a guide across the waters,
and even built monuments to align with her passing. Our earliest
ancestors turned their eyes upwards to the heavens in wonder as
they felt the ebb and flow within them and around them. Today,
in our modern world, we still ebb and flow with the moon's

tides, even if this realisation is only a distant memory, or even an inconvenience.

Within this book I offer an assortment of moon-related information that I have collected and worked with over the years, including the stories and folklore handed down from our ancestors as a means of explaining the moon's comings and goings, as well as poetry and ritualistic practices. This information has been organised in a manner to assist you should you desire to align yourself with the ever-changing cycles of that silvery orb that glides silently across the sky, waxing and waning in the heavens above us and within our lives as well.

Working with the moon can be likened to a voyage of self-discovery. Indeed, our emotions and feelings as well as our psychic and intuitive abilities are often attributed to the moon. The first section of this book focuses on exploring our connection with the moon through aligning our conscious self with the ebbing and flowing energies of the moon's 29½ day cycle. The second section outlines scientific facts about the moon and various lunar-related events. In the third section, we move deeper into moon magic with an assortment of offerings that you might like to include in your rituals with Lady Lunar. The fourth section contains an assortment of lunar correspondences and other associations that can enhance your lunar magic even further. The final section contains an assortment of other information, including rituals I have written for working with the moon.

Turn off your computer, put aside your mobile phone and step outside. Turn your gaze upwards to the heavens and close your eyes. Breathe and allow yourself to feel the pull of her lunar light, as the beams ebb and flow with her changing phases. Take a breath, dear reader, and gaze at Lady Lunar. She has many stories to tell you and many secrets to share as well.

Frances Billinghurst

In the Beginning

Queen and huntress, chaste and fair,
Now the sun is laid to sleep,
Seated in thy silver chair,
State in wonted manner keep:
Hesperus entreats thy light,
Goddess, excellently bright.

Earth, let not thy envious shade
Dare itself to interpose;
Cynthia's shining orb was made
Heaven to clear when day did close:
Bless us then with wished sight,
Goddess excellently bright.

Lay thy bow of pearl apart
And thy crystal-shining quiver;
Give unto the flying hart
Space to breathe, how short soever:
Thou that mak'st a day of night,
Goddess excellently bright.
('Cynthia's Revels' by Ben Jonson, c.1601)

To our early ancestors, the moon, our planet's only natural satellite, was the 'Land of the Gods' and a repository of the souls of the dead. It played centre stage in myths that explained the creation of the universe. It worked magic on Earth and on all living things under its cold light. Mysteriously, the tides rose and fell in rhythm with the moon. Unlike the sun, which was steady and constant in the sky, the moon was changeable, growing and diminishing in size, and yet it always looked upon Earth with the same enigmatic face.

Recorded observations of the moon date back to at least 1000 BCE, to the time of ancient Babylon (modern-day Iraq). Clay tablets were inscribed with cuneiform script and recorded the times and dates of when the moon rose and set, and the stars it passed, and even compared the rising and setting times of the moon with those of the sun. The information gained enabled Babylonians to construct lunar calendars that extended well into the future.[3] At some stage between 500 and 400 BCE, the Babylonians are believed to have identified and begun to use the 19-year cyclic relation between lunar months and solar years that today is known as the 'Metonic cycle'.[4]

In the 6th century BCE, Thales of Miletus, an early pre-Socratic philosopher and one of the so-called 'Seven Sages' of ancient Greece, was the first person to maintain that the moon had no light of its own and instead received and reflected that of the sun. From 300 BCE onwards, Hellenistic Stoic philosophers considered the moon a globe of fire and air.

In the 1st century, the Greek philosopher Plutarch (46–CE) believed the moon acted as a residence for the dead. In his essay 'On the Divine Vengeance', he mentioned that somewhere on the moon three daimons (spirits that the ancient Greeks placed somewhere between a human and a god) sat in a triangle mixing dreams in some kind of cosmic mixing bowl. He also considered that the moon was a portal through which spirits travelled on their way to being birthed on Earth.[5]

Ptolemy, the 2nd century Greco-Egyptian astronomer, explained the planetary movements in terms of an Earth-centred universe. He saw the moon as occupying the first orbit around Earth, followed by the sun and other planets visible to the naked eye. Today we know that Ptolemy was correct in determining that the moon revolves around Earth and is the closest planetary body; however, he was wrong about the sun and planets circling Earth. Nonetheless, his system was the accepted belief until Polish astronomer Nicolaus Copernicus (1473–1543) blew it apart with a sun-centred model. The Catholic Church at the time labelled this new theory heresy, yet the Copernican theory eventually proved itself.

Until the beginning of the 17th century, most European scientists and philosophers saw the universe almost exactly as described by the Greek philosopher Aristotle in the 3rd century BCE: that Earth was the corrupt, ever-changing realm of mortal life, and the celestial bodies were unchanging smooth, perfect spheres. It was the corruption of Earth that contaminated the moon, causing its changing surface colour as observed from below. This opinion was challenged in 1610 when Italian mathematician and astronomer Galileo Galilei published *Sidereus Nuncius*, in which he included the discoveries made through using his invention, a telescope. Noticing that the changing shadows of the moon occurred in correlation with the angle of the sunlight, he determined that, just like on Earth, the moon's surface had physical features on its surface that actually cast the shadows. Galileo was confirming a discovery made by Plutarch, who proposed many centuries earlier that the moon may have a terrain similar to that of Earth. Aristotle's view, however, had held sway until Galileo's observations challenged it.

Like Copernicus before him, Galileo's discovery, in particular that of Earth and moon orbiting around the sun, were not well received, especially by the powerful Catholic Church. The Roman Inquisition arrested and tried him in 1633. Galileo was subsequently found 'vehemently suspect of heresy' and placed under house arrest until his death on 8 January 1642. We have since learned that Galileo was correct; however, it took the Catholic Church some 359 years to formally admit their error when, on 31 October 1991, Pope John Paul II acknowledged that the Church erred in its condemnation of the astronomer.[6]

In the 17th century, Sir Isaac Newton used the moon to test his theory of motion and mechanics. The mathematician, physicist and astronomer discovered that ocean tides resulted from the gravitational attraction of the sun and moon on the Earth's surface.

In more recent times, it has been discovered that during the elliptical journey that our moon (the fifth largest in our solar system) takes around Earth, it is some 363,300 kms (225,700 miles) at its closest approach (known as a 'perigee') and 384,400 kms (238,855 miles) at its furthest approach (known as an 'apogee'). These terms come into effect when people talk about 'super' or 'micro' moons, which are discussed in Part I of this book. It has also been discovered that the moon travels at an average speed of around 3,680 km per hour (2,287 mph) around our planet. Still, there is much to learn about her.

Moon as a Timekeeper

Early humankind understood that the sun gave life and without it, things perished. However, the moon was believed to regulate life and was a timekeeper. In 1911, an archaeological discovery was made in south-western France of a limestone bas-relief that depicted a naked female form holding a curved horn. This relief, known as the Venus of Laussel, was painted with red ochre on the limestone of the rock shelter, and dated back to around 22,000 BCE. The horn, which had 13 vertical lines etched on it, has been interpreted as being related to the 13 lunar months that occur in one solar year. With the hand placed on the stomach, some people have also interpreted the image as relating to a woman's menstrual cycle, which is often in alignment with the moon. Whichever is the more correct interpretation, we may never know.

The female menstrual cycle has always aroused a degree of curiosity. Maybe it is because of its connection with the moon? Away from the influence of the city and artificial lighting, even today, women tend to menstruate on or around the full (or dark) moon. It is believed that in ancient cultures, menstruation huts were provided for women to retreat to during their times of bleeding. Here, they would focus on their inner power, for it was during this time that a woman's psychic abilities were believed to be at their most potent. Over the centuries, this belief has led to a number of taboos against menstruation, some of which can still be observed today. They reflect how menstruation, a very natural process, is still deemed as 'unclean', or called 'the curse', and women are still made to feel as if they are inadequate, somewhat weakened or even shamed during this time of the month.

It is interesting to note that the word 'menstruation' or *me(n) ses* is considered an Indo-English word meaning 'moon, month' (sharing a similar meaning with the Sanskrit *masah*), the Greek *mene* 'moon', *men* 'month' and the Latin *mensis* 'month'. Likewise, it is connected to the old Proto-Germanic word **menoth-*, which also means 'moon'. Another word connected with the moon is 'Monday', the name for the first day of the working week. This is derived from the old English *Mōnandæg* and Middle English *Monenday* meaning 'moon day', both of which are translations of late Latin *lunae dies* ('day of the moon'). Within esoteric and more magical circles, Monday is viewed as being ruled by the moon.

It is not only a woman's menstrual cycle that the moon is believed to regulate but also the other tides. It is the moon's gravitational pull on Earth that causes the levels of the oceans to rise and fall, a phenomenon that we refer to as 'tides'. High tides occur when the pull of the moon causes the water to bulge upwards. This also happens on the side of Earth farthest from the moon owing to the inertia of water. When the water drops, this is the low tide. It occurs between the two high tidal humps. This ebbing and flowing of tides also occur in lakes, the atmosphere and even within Earth's crust, only to a much smaller extent. As humans, we are composed of a large percentage of water (some 70–80%); the moon affects us by pulling on our inner tides just as it does with the seas and oceans around us.

NASA scientists have discovered that the pull of the moon is having a gradual slowing effect on Earth's rotation, an effect referred to as 'tidal braking'. This means that the length of our days is increasing by 2.3 milliseconds per century. While this may not seem much, over time, its impact could very well be felt; any energy Earth loses is retrieved by the moon, enabling our lunar orb to increase its distance by some 3.8 cm (1.5 inches). This is important because it is moon's gravitational pull on Earth that makes our planet liveable. This pull moderates the degree of wobble that occurs because of Earth's axial tilt, which has resulted in the establishment of a relatively stable climate over billions of years. The further the moon moves away from Earth, the lesser its effect on our planet.

Our early ancestors often considered the moon the 'Universal Mother' and the 'Queen of Heaven', who symbolised the absolute principle of femininity, spirituality and fertility. The moon was believed to make all things grow and governed all life-giving moisture. Its changing phases were associated with the coming of rain and with the torrents that produced floods. Its fertilising power governed not only plants and animals but, at one stage, humans as well. Women who slept beneath the rays of the moon would become impregnated by them, or so it was once thought. As early humankind developed what we term today folklore and mythology, the deities associated with water, fertility and fecundity were often also associated with the moon. This belief was somewhat proven in the mid-1950s when Slovakian doctor Eugen Jonas allegedly discovered an ancient Assyrian astrological text that indicated women were at their most fertile during certain phases of the moon. He went on to frame an entire family planning method around this hypothesis, advising patients that they ovulated when the moon was in the same position as when they were born.[7]

With the discovery of agriculture and animal husbandry, the lunar cycle became a guide for the planting and harvesting of crops as well as the slaughter of animals. The gods and goddesses overseeing these activities invariably had lunar associations.

Deities ascribed healing functions were also associated with the moon. One reason for this was that the moon was perceived to govern all the moisture within the body and the external world. Rites to influence these aspects of life were addressed to the moon and to the moon's representatives in the forms of these gods and goddesses.

Because of the moon's apparent rebirth in the sky every month, the moon became, in many cosmologies, the repository of souls after death. As mentioned previously, in the 1st century, Plutarch conceived the moon to be a lunar waystation for the going and coming of souls. He believed that humans had two deaths. The first occurred on Earth, the domain of Demeter, the Greek Goddess of Fecundity, when the body was severed from the mind and soul, and returned to the dust. The soul and psyche then went to the moon, the domain of Persephone, the Queen of the Underworld, where a second death took place with the separation of the two. The soul returned to the substance of the moon, where it was able to retain the dreams and memories of the life that had been lived. The mind, meanwhile, went to the sun, where it was absorbed and then gave birth to a new soul. In rebirth, the process was reversed; the sun sent the mind to the moon, where it was joined with the soul, then travelled to Earth to join the body and be born anew.

In 1961, the then US president, John F. Kennedy, declared that he wanted humans to land on the moon. Eight years later, on 20 July 1969, Neil Armstrong, Edwin 'Buzz' Aldrin and Michael Collins blasted off as part of the Apollo 11 space mission, during which Armstrong become the first moon walker. Despite other landings having occurred since this mission, there are some people today who still question whether the initial moonwalk actually happened.

Today, Lady Lunar continues to be a focus of fascination. Science fiction writers have long fantasised about an assortment of beings residing on the moon. She has also drawn the unwanted attention of big corporations interested in obtaining mining speculation rights to expose the potential secrets that may be contained deep under her surface. Governments and entrepreneurs even play with the idea of whether we can populate her should our own planet become unliveable. All the while, she continues to ebb and flow, silently affecting us on Earth.

Part I
Cycles of Change

Daughters of Jove, whose voice is melody,
Muses, who know and rule all minstrelsy
Sing the wide-winged Moon! Around the earth,
From her immortal head in Heaven shot forth,
Far light is scattered – boundless glory springs;
Where'er she spreads her many-beaming wings
The lampless air glows round her golden crown.

But when the Moon divine from Heaven is gone
Under the sea, her beams within abide,
Till, bathing her bright limbs in Ocean's tide,
Clothing her form in garments glittering far,
And having yoked to her immortal car
The beam-invested steeds whose necks on high
Curve back, she drives to a remoter sky
A western Crescent, borne impetuously.
Then is made full the circle of her light,
And as she grows, her beams more bright and bright
Are poured from Heaven, where she is hovering then,
A wonder and a sign to mortal men.

The Son of Saturn with this glorious Power
Mingled in love and sleep – to whom she bore
Pandeia, a bright maid of beauty rare
Among the Gods, whose lives eternal are.
Hail Queen, great Moon, white-armed Divinity,
Fair-haired and favourable! thus with thee
My song beginning, by its music sweet
Shall make immortal many a glorious feat
Of demigods, with lovely lips, so well
Which minstrels, servants of the Muses, tell.
('Ode to the Moon' by Percy Bysshe Shelley[8])

The Eight Phases of the Moon

O Lady Moon, your horns point toward the east;
Shine, be increased:
O Lady Moon, your horns point toward the west;
Wane, be at rest.
(From *Sing-Song* by Christina Georgina Rossetti[9])

The moon is one of the most important heavenly bodies within esoteric practices. The phases that it goes through during the month are considered when rituals and other magical workings are performed. This is because each phase contains different energies that are believed to affect the outcome of rituals and spell work. As humans, we are made up of between 50% and 70% water and as the moon governs watery bodies such as the ocean tides, the moon also governs our own inner tides. While this is more noticeable in women (menstrual cycles), the moon also pulls the tides in men.

The connection between the moon and our planet was mentioned in an opening address made by Professor Cesare Barbieni marking the 400th anniversary of Galileo's astronomical breakthrough. In this address at the Galilean Academy of Sciences Literature and Arts at the University of Padua, Italy, where Galileo made his pioneering breakthrough in the area of astronomy, Professor Barbieni noted the importance of understanding the relationship between the moon and our own planet.

The earth harbours life, the moon is extremely sterile, however our natural satellite regulates the life, through the stability of the terrestrial rotational axis, through the tides and perhaps through subtler effects that still need to be better understood.

Therefore, the study of the moon and of its relationship with the earth should be of highest priority.[10]

Within more Earth-centric spiritualties, this revelation is of no surprise. As indicated in the previous section, our ancestors have long believed that there was a connection not only between the moon and our planet but also between the moon and Earth's inhabitants as it progresses through its different phases, each causing cycles of change.

The face of the moon comes and goes each month, a process of waxing and waning known as the lunar phases. The new moon, which starts the cycle, is virtually invisible. In the days that follow, the moon reveals more and more of itself as it makes its journey around Earth. Halfway through the cycle, the moon is completely illuminated. From this point onwards, the process reverses and the moon, now in its waning phase, grows darker and darker until it seemingly disappears from view completely. A few days later, the moon reappears and the whole cycle begins all over again.

The phases of the moon are caused by the relative positions of the Earth, sun and moon. It takes an average of 27.3 days for the moon to rotate around Earth. This measurement is relative to the stars and is called the sidereal, or 'orbital', period. However, because of Earth's rotation around the sun, to earthbound observers (i.e. us), a complete moon cycle appears to take a couple of days longer: 29.5305882 days to be exact. This number is called the synodic period, or 'lunation', and is relative to the sun. The changing positions of the sun, Earth and moon are known as the 'synodic month' (from the Greek *synods* meaning 'session').

The sun always illuminates the half of the moon facing the sun (except during lunar eclipses when the moon passes through Earth's shadow, resulting in the light being seen from Earth). When the sun and moon are on opposite sides of Earth, the moon appears 'full' to us – a bright, round disc. When the moon is between the Earth and the sun, it appears dark. In between, the moon's illuminated surface appears to grow (wax) to full, then decreases (wanes) to the next dark (new) moon.

In 1967 American astrologer, Dane Rudhyar, divided the motions of the moon into eight main phases, which are indicated in the following diagram. Since Rudhyar's division of the moon's cycle, nearly everyone who works with the moon, especially from an astrological perspective, has used his work, although some of the names used for the differing phases may have changed.

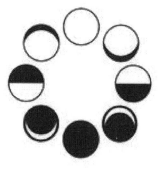

Figure 1 – Moon Phases

The cycle begins when the moon is lined up directly between the sun and Earth, and therefore is virtually invisible. As the moon begins to move away from the sun, the waxing crescent shape appears – a sliver of light on the right side in the Northern Hemisphere (☽), which is the symbol that is used in calendars. However, if you reside south of the equator, in the Southern Hemisphere, as I do, then the sliver of light appears on the left side of the moon (☾). As the moon continues to wax, the light will grow over its surface from right to left (in the Northern Hemisphere) or left to right (in the Southern Hemisphere).

By the time the moon is half lit, it has completed one-quarter of its journey around Earth, which is why it is said to be in its 'first quarter'. As the moon continues to grow brighter, it reaches the waxing gibbous phase when it is three-quarters full. Finally, it becomes fully illuminated, or a full moon. The above diagram shows the moon in relation to the sun and Earth from a Northern Hemispheric perspective. For the Southern Hemisphere, as mentioned previously, the waxing and waning crescent should be depicted facing the other way.

With the moon on the opposite the side of Earth from where it began as a new moon, from this point on the moon is in its waning phase. Darkness descends from left to right. A dark crescent appears on the left side, marking the waning gibbous phase (appearing as ☾ in the night's sky in the Northern Hemisphere and ☽ in the Southern Hemisphere). Next comes the last quarter, when the moon is half dark. In its last phase, the only visible light is in a crescent shape on its right side. Finally, the moon reaches the phase of the new moon again. The moon takes approximately 3.5 days to move through each stage.

I should point out that there is a slight difference between the perceptions of the moon phases of an astrologer and the perceptions of those who are more esoteric, or occult, influenced. I personally fall into the second category because I recognise an additional 'phase' of the moon, that of the dark moon. I also work with the exact timings of the dark and full moons to ensure that I capture the energy at their peak instead of over a three-day period. All this will be explained later in this book. If astrology is your drawcard when it comes to working with the moon, I would recommend that you include more astrology-based books and websites in your study. The more familiar you become with working with the lunar energies, the more observant you will become of the differences between all eight phases (or nine as in my case).

Working with the Moon

A new moon rises with the sun
Its waxing half at midday shows,
The full moon climbs at sunset hour,
And waning half the midnight knows.
(Author Unknown)

The never-ending cycles of the moon are one of the most fundamental and readily observable rhythms of the natural world. We flow with the currents of the moon whether we are conscious of them or not, as recorded in the above country rhyme.

In the tarot, the moon card relates to introspection, about reflecting back at ourselves the life that we want to be living. The moon after all reflects the sun's light because it had no light of its own. Therefore, this part of the book is largely about introspection, of going inwards and finding ways to nurture and nourish the soul. It is about (re)connecting with the moon and its gentle ebbing and flowing on our lives.

When we work with the moon, it may very well reveal to us what we already know. Do you find that you are more restless at times during certain phases of the moon? At Basel University in Switzerland, research found that it was not uncommon for people to take longer to fall asleep, to sleep less or even to sleep lighter during a full moon. How this actually happens, however, has not been determined, but it may have something to do with the gravitational pull that the moon has on our bodies. Other common experiences during the full moon include intense or more active dreams, increased feelings of restlessness, bursts of inspiration, hypersensitivity or even headaches and feeling energetically drained. If you notice that you experience any of these symptoms more during certain times of the month than others, it could very well be due to the moon. One way to gain more insight is to consciously work with the different phases as I suggest here.

This section of the book is purposely divided into each of the main phases of the moon – the new, waxing, full and waning, as well as the mysterious dark moon. I have combined the three waxing phases together, and likewise the three waning phases. This is to enable you, the reader, to read along with each phase, explore what it means to you on a deeper, more soul-purposed level and to record your discoveries, especially if you have undertaken any of the activities and rituals that are provided. It is through the recording of your own discoveries that you are able to unblock your truest potential and nature.

Lunar Journaling

If you have never worked with the moon before, you might like to begin by reading each section during the appropriate moon phase and keeping a journal or diary of your experiences. This will assist you in your alignment with the moon through the unlocking of your true potential. Remember that the moon reflects back to you the key needed to manifest the life you desire.

Before moving on with this section, you need the following objects:

- A journal or blank diary, notebook or an exercise book to record your lunar journeys.
- A white candle (this can be a taper, votive or even a tealight) with a suitable candle holder (silver or glass preferred). You may like to light your white candle each night while you write in your journal, perform your meditations or simply gaze at the moon.

An optional item is a small dark-coloured bowl that you can hold comfortably in your hands. This bowl will serve as a vessel for water and will often be used to reflect the moon back at you. The bowl I use was purchased in an artist studio; however, you can find a suitable one in a second-hand charity shop, flea market or your own cupboard.

The final thing you will need when working with Lady Lunar is an open heart and mind. Many of the myths and meditations that follow may be unfamiliar to you. They have been specifically chosen, however, to inspire your soul and concentrate your inner yearning to connect more with Lady Lunar.

The purpose of creating a lunar journal is to record your intentions, musings, aspirations and thoughts about what you would like to manifest, as well as habits and other aspects about your personality, or things and situations that occur in your life that you wish to banish or remove. Through the act of writing, we make ourselves accountable by transferring our thoughts and feelings from our mind onto paper, where they materialise.

Just as the moon renews itself every 29.5 days, so too can you through recommitting to self-improvement. After all, this is what the process of journaling or keeping a true reflection diary is all about. Where you start with your lunar observances is entirely up to you. For ease, I have started at the new moon, when the first sliver appears in the sky. However, if the moon is full or waning, you may wish to commence reading at that appropriate section. It does not really matter what phase you commence your journaling and observances – what does matter is that you start.

If the whole concept of journaling is new to you, keep in mind that there is no right or wrong way to do this work. What I offer in the following pages are largely starting points, or prompts, to assist you in connecting with the moon. If you are not a writer, then use dot points or include images from magazines or downloaded from the internet, your own doodles and so on that reflect your thoughts. As you progress through the lunar cycle, I am confident the more familiar you become with this work, the easier it will become. Each lunar cycle can build upon the previous one as you progress through the year and as with all kinds of journaling work, it is often at a later date that your journey with the moon and how it affects your life will become more evident to you. So, let us begin.

The New Moon

The new moon of no importance
lingers behind as the yellow ungloves
and is gone beyond the sea's edge
earth smokes blue;
the new moon, in cool height above the bushes
brings a fresh fragrance of heaven to our senses.
(D.H. Lawrence, 1885–1930)

From when the first sliver appears in the night's sky until about 3.5 days later, this is the time of the new moon, and the commencement of the lunar cycle. The moon and sun are on the same degree of the zodiac. During these three days, the lunar orb moves from 0° to 45° ahead of the sun, rising at dawn and setting just after dusk.

The appearance of the returning lunar orb after complete darkness reminds us that now is the perfect time to start planning and focusing on what we want to bring into our lives, that while anything is possible, we need to make a start. With this first sliver of the new moon, now is the time to decide what it is that we truly want to bring into manifestation. Is it a new project, a new attitude or even a direction in life that we wish to take? The new moon also reminds us that now is the time for renewal, providing us with the necessary energy that will aid us in accepting or attempting change in our lives.

Begin your new moon journaling by drawing freehand the image of the new moon in your journal. If you reside in the Northern Hemisphere, the horns of the new moon point to the left ☽. However, if you reside in the Southern Hemisphere, the horns point to the right ☾. Light your white candle and try to sit where you can see the new moon as you contemplate each of the following questions in turn, writing your insights in your journal:

- What are your intentions, musings or aspirations for this coming lunar cycle?
- What new beginnings do you wish to make?
- How will you encourage these new beginnings?
- Are there any areas you wish to change in your life?
- What inspires creativity within you?
- What is your heartfelt desire?
- Do you have any dreams that keep repeating? If so, what do you feel is the message of these dreams?

Because no one else needs to see or know what is written in your lunar journal, except for Lady Lunar, it can become your own personal manifesto of experiences. The truth found through accurately recording your thoughts, hopes and even fears will only ever be revealed to you, enabling you to see the patterns locked deep within your soul more clearly. Journaling does not have to involve long-winded accounts. As mentioned previously, it can consist of simple dot points, drawings or even quotations from the internet that resonate with you.

When the first sliver of silvery light appears in the night's sky, we are like a blank canvas of the lunar cycle, so what possibilities do you wish to achieve? What do you want to bring into your life? What do you want to manifest?

Now is also a perfect time to review your life and weigh up what you have achieved, or have yet to achieve, to date. It is all about new beginnings; this is why many people prefer to commence tasks and projects at the new moon, in that as the moon increases in size so too does the energy delivered to those particular tasks or projects. You may even like to do some soul searching, especially if you are not satisfied with your current circumstances or direction that your life seems to be heading in. You might like to ask yourself:

- What do I really want?
- What do I really need?
- Where do I really want to go?

As you think about your goals, consider how you are going to achieve them, what steps need to be taken, what do you need to focus on to be able to gain a clearer picture in your own mind and, therefore, a more accurate vision that you can truly believe in. By answering the above three questions, you will gain a deeper level of insight into what you wish to achieve, not to mention your own ability and commitment to any possible change or new direction. What are you true feelings about your dreams and desires – are they just that? Or are they things that you actually truly wish to achieve and are prepared to invest energy into?

The new moon also offers a perfect time to celebrate what you have been able to accomplish to date. Too often we tend to focus on what we have not achieved or what is missing from our lives, as opposed to what we actually have and what we often take for granted. This is very much 'the grass is always greener' type scenario.

Planning for the New Moon

What goal do you wish to achieve that you have not yet accomplished? Consider what first steps are needed to help you fulfil this goal. As the Buddha stated, there are many ways to climb a mountain, but they all start with the first step. List the steps that you can achieve and what needs to be done to achieve the other steps. Do you need to undertake additional study or attend a course to gain the knowledge needed?

You may like to construct your own manifestation or vision board in addition to your journal. Basically, these boards are a collection of pictures, phrases or symbols that represent what you wish to bring or manifest into your life. They can also include positive phrases or affirmations to reinforce your desires. The board is then displayed somewhere where you can see it often as a reminder to keep focusing on the realisation of your dreams and desires. I prefer to make vision boards on A3-sized card but A4 paper or even within your lunar journal is perfectly fine. If it is within your journal, just remember that you need to keep focusing on it throughout the lunar cycle.

You can arrange your images in a manner that is pleasing for you during the new moon. Once your board is completed, you might like to light your white candle and offer your vision board up to the moon. As you do, recite the following prayer of manifestation, or another one that you feel represents your wishes:

Lady Lunar of the silvery light
Shining from the sky at night
Grant my wishes and mind be clear
I flourish and grow when you are near
Lady Lunar of the silvery light
Grant me a boon with your purifying light.

Too often we focus on the negative or what is missing from our lives instead of the positive and what we have. You might like to set positive intentions during the new moon by making a list of positive statements or attributes about yourself. While the number is not important, what is important is the ability to be able to think positively about yourself. You can always add to your list of positive things. Consider how you word your statements. Can they be rewritten to sound more positive? Do they clearly reflect what you desire?

New Moon Ritual

I love writing and performing rituals. Therefore, the ones I perform can often be rather elaborate. Having said that, delight can also be found in something extremely simplistic. As the new moon offers a blank page and the means for a fresh start when we can spend time to turn inward and consider what we want to call into our lives, this can also be reflected in the rituals we undertake. The following is a suggestion of what you may like to use or incorporate into your own lunar rites for the new moon:

- Create a sacred space: A white or silver piece of cloth or a special moon altar cloth can be used to adorn a flat surface that you will use as your altar. Alternatively, you can put a tapestry on the floor or even mark an area in whatever manner appeals to you. Place on your altar a new white (or silver) candle in either a silver or clear glass holder, and your bowl of fresh water. If you like scent, you can add your chosen preference (i.e. incense or essential oils). Likewise, you may have other items you wish to add to your moon. I would suggest, however, that because this phase is basically marking the preliminary process, the simpler the altar is the better. When I am about to commence my rite, I light my candle and incense, and then spend a few moments grounding and centring through focusing on my breath, breathing deep into my abdomen to calm my mind and enable me to focus on what I am about to undertake.
- Create a connection to the energies that you feel most connected with. These could be your spirit guides, ancestors, angels or even your higher consciousness. I personally like to connect with the four elements (earth, air, fire and water) as well as a lunar deity. A detailed list of lunar deities can be found later in this book. A simple connection with the elements can be as follows:

I call on the element of earth that is my body.
It connects me to the land upon which I live,

its vitality and all the abundance of life.
I call on the element of fire that is my blood.
It pumps throughout my body,
connecting me to the sacred flame that ignites my passion.
I call on the element of water that is my tears,
It flows throughout my body through my fluids and emotions,
connecting me to the psychic realms.
I call on the element of air that is my breath,
It moves through my thoughts and mental processes,
connecting me to the inspiration of all things.

- The following invocation is designed to assist you to align with Lady Lunar on a more general basis. Before I recite the invocation, I visualise the moon above me in the night's sky with the rays streaming down, entering my physical body through the top of my head (my crown chakra). If I wish to further align with a particular lunar deity (such as one from the list of such deities I have included in Part IV of this book), I try to have an image of that particular deity available on my altar space. These days you can easily obtain a suitable picture from the internet.

Lady Lunar of the midnight skies
Shine down your wisdom from up high
Nourish my soul with your mysteries
Uplift my spirit with your majesty.
Lady Lunar, grant me my boon
Queen of my heart, Lady Moon.

- Sit comfortably and write in your journal what your intentions are for the coming lunar cycle. What things would you like to bring into your life? These could be a job opportunity, a relationship, financial abundance or even an adventure.

- Speak aloud each intention that you have written down. Vocalising helps to bring them into manifestation. You may notice that they evoke even more emotion when spoken out loud.
- Place the bowl of water where you can see the reflection of the moon in it. Meditate and contemplate. Sit quietly, follow your breath and visualise your desires coming to fruition. Set the intention to stay open to experiences entering your life and any other growth opportunities you may need along the way.
- You may like to end your ritual by reading and contemplating the words of the following, which have been adapted from a poem by 13th century Persian poet Rumi, which I feel relates to the awakening of potential, in other words, the new moon:

If you never searched for truth come with us and you will become a seeker.
If you were never a musician come with us and you will find your voice.
In our gathering one candle lights hundreds
We will light your path and give you courage
So you will open like a flower and join in joyous laughter.
Plant the seed of truth and watch it grow when it spreads its branches
Come with us and sit under the blossoms.
Your eyes will open to the secret of the truth.

- When you are ready, close your circle and open your sacred space. If I have called in the elements and a lunar deity, then I thank them and bid that they depart. If I have used a tealight candle, I let it burn out. Any larger candle, such as a taper, I extinguish and then light the same candle over the following lunar cycle. You may, however, prefer to burn the candle for a couple of hours every night during the waxing phase of the lunar cycle, ensuring that the candle is always placed in a safe place (i.e. in the kitchen sink, where it will not be knocked over).

Do not be surprised if you notice an onslaught of new ideas during the days leading up to and following the new moon, or a burst of creative energy and even physical energy. You may also like to make note of how your emotions and body respond to each moon phase and whether you can use this information to your advantage. In Part III, you will find a lunar chart that can assist you with this.

Prayer for the New Moon

When you see the first sliver of the moon in the night's sky, you might like to recite this Scottish Gaelic traditional folk prayer[11] to the new moon (or use it as inspiration to write your own):

Greeting to you, New Moon, kindly jewel of guidance!
I bend my knees to you, I offer you my love
I bend my knees to you, I raise my hands to you
I lift up my eyes to you, New Moon of the Seasons.
Greeting to you, New Moon, darling of my love!
Greeting to you, New Moon, darling of graces,
You journey on your course, you steer the flood tides,
You light up your face for us, New Moon of the Seasons.
Queen of guidance, queen of good luck, queen of my love,
New Moon of the Seasons!

Greeting to you, gem of the night
Beauty of the skies, gem of the night
Mother of the stars, gem of the night
Foster-child of the sun, gem of the night
Majesty of the stars, gem of the night.

Magical New Moon Workings

During this time, the combination of solar and lunar energies can provide strength to new projects. Any spells, magical workings or any other kind of ceremony performed during this time should focus on self-improvement, employment, health, farms, gardens and romance.

Some people use the time frame of new moon to new moon. I prefer to use astrological influences (which I discuss in Part II under Astrological Keys). By this, I mean that if the new moon is in Aries, then I allow my magic the opportunity to manifest by the time the full moon in Aries arrives. However, at the end of the day, there is really no right or wrong way of manifesting magic.

The Waxing Moons
(Crescent, First Quarter, Gibbous)

All night have the roses heard
The flute, violin, bassoon;
All night has the casement jessamine stirr'd
To the dancers dancing in turn;
Till silence fell with the waking bird,
And a hush with the setting moon.
('Come into the Garden, Maud' by Lord Alfred Tennyson)

After the first sliver of the new moon has appeared in the sky, Lady Lunar steadily increases in size each night. When the sun sets and the sky darkens, the waxing crescent appears in view in the western sky, where it rises an hour to several hours behind the sun. There are three phases of the waxing moon – the waxing crescent (from 3.5 to 6 days after the first sliver of the new moon), the first quarter (from 6 to 9.5 days from the new moon) and the waxing gibbous (from 10 to 13.5 days from the new moon). This steady increase in the size of the moon encourages us to focus on the manifestation of dreams and projects, as well as thoughts and adventures.

The more we can connect with her essence, the stronger the lunar energy flows through us and into everything that we do. Just as the ocean's tides ebb and flow to the rhythm of the moon, so too do we, even if we are not consciously aware of it. The more we focus on these tides, the easier it is for us to tap into the ever-changing rhythms. Therefore, when we tap into the energies of the waxing crescent moon, we realise that now is the time to focus on invocations, attraction and the bringing of abundance or manifestation into our life.

Waxing Crescent Moon

As the moon becomes more visible, increasing in size and brightness, moving from 45° to 90° ahead of the sun, our visons, dreams and intentions become goals and plans as they too solidify. The momentum begins to build; we begin to see and feel the information needed as our dreams start to manifest. The increasing brightness of the moon illuminates the direction we need to follow once the path itself is found.

Above us in the night's sky, the slender crescent of Lady Lunar is becoming more visible as she reflects the intangible ideas and inspirations. The waxing crescent moon is the time for seeking and developing. We become more and more aware of how our vision needs to evolve as we ascertain the possible from the impossible, gathering our resources. We encounter the reality of what it takes to make our vision, goal or dream manifest.

The moon can also highlight possible complications and stresses as we become aware of the amount of effort that may be needed to bring our dreams into manifestation. Doubts and second thoughts may arise. Do we actually have the commitment? Are we capable of making a conscious effort to maintain and continue building the momentum to push forward, easing the self-doubt? Sceptical people may also appear in our lives, making it easier for us to give up on achieving our dreams and goals, especially if we encounter glitches. During the waxing crescent moon, we will experience many challenges; we will need to draw upon our inner strength and trust ourselves. We will need to stand up to criticism, using any negative energy that we receive as a force to push forward.

Be mindful that self-doubt can make it easy to fall back into bad habits or take the easier option. When you encounter such doubt or hesitancy, focus on the vision board or the list of goals that you compiled at the new moon. Remind yourself why you created these goals in the first place, and why they are important to you. As you reflect back, ask yourself:

- Why have I chosen this particular goal?
- Why is this goal so important to me?

Reclaim that inner fire of determination. Remind yourself of the desire and the need your goals and visions will fulfil once attained.

As the moon grows in shape, its energy builds and this is what we feel during this phase, the beginnings of solidity. Our focus leads to the formation and the evolution towards manifestation. To keep our focus and vision clear, we must ensure that the path we follow is also clear. Now is the time for developing the energy we have gathered as we turn our ideas into plans and become more and more aware of how the vision must evolve. In doing this, we sort out the possible from the impossible.

While our intangible ideas and inspirations are taking form, this opens the way for complications, commitments and even second thoughts as we are tested to see how dedicated and true to our vision we actually are. We need to actively push forward and make a conscious effort to maintain and build momentum. Inner doubts, sceptical people and other distractions offer us a way out and challenge our inner strength, our determination and our trust in our own ability. If you find yourself in such a place, focus on the moon and the journal entries that you have made that explain why you are seeking this manifestation. Remember that the fragile crescent of the moon lasts only for a short while before it becomes more and more solid. So too will your desire. As it steadily increases, so too does our ability to manifest. Therefore, look to the moon for the promised growth and know that within yourself, your efforts are able to hold up to the vast darkness.

It is not the time to procrastinate. It is the time to forge ahead and to ensure that your new moon ideas take root. It is a good time for gathering and analysing resources, commencing study or projects, and creating new and more positive habits.

You may even find yourself busier than normal. If this happens, pay attention to your stress management. While it is not a good time to give things up, keep in mind that you do not need to attempt to do everything at once. Challenges will develop; however, you do not need to become a workaholic. Take a deep breath when needed. Decide what you are capable of completing. Remember that the important thing at the moment is to develop and maintain confidence and determination in yourself and your ability.

The waxing crescent moon is the time to begin to pull things together and take small steps. When you have been scattering resources and focus, or even have veered off track, use this time to step back on track. It is also an appropriate time to begin to make longer termed plans that will set you up in the future.

Waxing Crescent Moon Manifestation

As Lady Lunar begins to increase in size, now is the perfect time to focus on manifesting or bringing things into our lives. This can include starting new adventures or initiating new projects, increasing personal health or wealth prospects (i.e. a new job or career) or bringing new love into your life.

For the following manifestation ritual, you will need your lunar journal or notebook, a pen, a candle and matches or a lighter to light it with and some incense.

If you have performed rituals before, you can commence using whatever format you normally use. You can follow the format given earlier in the New Moon section in which the elements are called in, or you can follow the very simple format outlined below:

- Light your candle, and if you use incense, light that as well. Close your eyes and spend the next few moments simply following your breath. As you inhale, you may like to visualise that you are breathing in a healing golden or silvery light that circulates throughout your body, and as you exhale, you breathe out a murky-coloured light that represents any stress or anxiety you may be feeling, or things that are no longer needed or wanted in your life. As you continue to simply inhale and exhale, you may notice that your breathing deepens (i.e. you begin to breathe into your diaphragm as opposed to the top of your lungs). As this happens, your physical body will relax more and more.

- Bring your awareness back to the here and now. In your lunar journal or notebook write the statement 'I accept these things into my life from this point forward'.

- Under this statement, list your desires, all the things you wish to bring into your life. You may only have one thing, or you may have many. The quantity does not matter. What does matter, however, is that you ensure that you truly want all of the things that you have listed. If you wish to gain a better paying and more satisfactory job, then consider the qualifications or experience that you already possess because it might be better to focus on undertaking additional study first. If you desire a relationship, it is often far better to list the attributes of a person than an actual person's name. If you want more money, consider how this money is to be received. Remember the initial statement that you have written, 'I accept these things into my life from this point forward'. This statement can be likened to making a contract with Lady Lunar with which you are going to hold yourself responsible. With this in mind, you may wish to revisit your list.

- When you are happy with all of the items on your manifestation list, state the following:

Lady Lunar, whose light is the first I see
I ask that you bring my desires to me

As your light grows so perfectly
Grant me your boon, so mote it be.

- As you recite your list of desires out loud by stating 'By the waxing light of the moon, I manifest …'. Listen to the statements carefully as you speak them, ensuring that they truly resonate with you before moving on to the next desire. If you feel that any of the statements do not resonate, you might want to rewrite them, or it could simply not be the right time for that desire to be put into the cycle of manifestation.

- During the following lunar cycle, when a listed desire has been achieved, rewrite your list to ensure that the only items listed are those that are still relevant and appropriate to you. When you rewrite the list, you may find that you need to reword some of the original phrases so that they align more with your current thinking. Keep in mind that it is perfectly natural to change your mind should you find that a desire on your list no longer applies.

Candle Manifestation

An additional step in the above manifestation exercise occurs after you have decided what you want to bring into your life at the new moon. Take a new pillar candle and either hold it in your hands or have it in front of you as you meditate on your intent. See yourself having achieved your desire, ensuring that this visualisation resonates properly with you. Alternatively, you might like to rewrite your desire.

When you are ready, take a sharp object (i.e. a knife, toothpick or even a sharp pencil), and carefully carve words or an image that represents your desire into the candle. For example, if your desire relates to financial gain, you could draw a dollar sign. I often find it beneficial to have an actual use for that financial gain, such as a new car, that will enable me to begin work. Therefore, a more direct image would be a dollar sign drawn inside an image of a car. If your goal is love, a heart can be drawn; if it is study, maybe a graduation hat can be drawn. Simplicity tends to work best. There are, however, more specific and somewhat complicated magical practices used by some people with the construction of symbols, which are also referred to as 'sigils'. I find the above method, using somewhat simplistic imagery, works just as well.

The choice of candle that you use is up to you. Candles made from 100% soy wax, although very popular, may not be an appropriate choice for inscribing sigils. This is because soy is a very soft form of wax that does not hold its own, which is why 100% soy candles are only found in some kind of container. If I am using a soy candle, I write or draw my desire on a piece of paper and place it under the candle while it burns. In such an instance you do not need to anoint or dress a soy candle (which I discuss below). If you prefer to use taper or pillar candles, these are more often than not made from paraffin or a paraffin blend wax.

A further point I should mention is that the colour of the candle and choice of oil and herbs with which you dress the candle can also add to your magical working. I provided a list of suitable colours and herbal correspondences in my previous book, *Contemporary Witchcraft: Foundation Practices for a Magical Life*, so I do not want to repeat that information here. I have included some resources at the end of this book, not to mention that a simple search on the internet will also produce such information. Rule of thumb, however, is to use a white candle if in doubt. I always ensure I have a few normal household candles on hand just in case I do not have an appropriately coloured candle.

Once you have your candle, the next step is to anoint it with an appropriate oil or candle-conditioning oil and dress it in herbs. To draw energies to you, put a small amount of oil on your fingers and, starting from the top (wick end), stroke the oil to the middle of the candle. Ensure that you do not spill any oil on the wick. If this happens, you might have difficulties lighting the candle. Then, repeat the process, stroking oil from the base of the candle to the middle. You can use a similar method to anoint candles during the waning phases of the moon to remove energies from you by reversing the directions (i.e. starting at the middle of the candle and stroking down to the base or up to the top). Once it is prepared, place the candle in an appropriate candle holder. I provide some simple yet effective oil recipes in Part III of this book.

If you have selected some herbs to add further power to your manifestation, while ensuring that they are not toxic when burned, roll your oiled candle into the herbs, adding a bit of pressure to enable the herbs to stick to the candle. Once it is dressed, place your candle in an appropriate candle holder.

Prepare your space as mentioned in the New Moon section or in Part V. When you are ready, light your candle and speak your words of manifestation. As mentioned previously, by vocalising the words as opposed to thinking them, the vibration of the spoken word tends to help us hold greater accountability.

Visualise yourself having already achieved your goal. Repeat your chant until you feel the energies rise and then direct them into the candle. When you have done this, sit and breathe deeply into your solar plexus (also known by its Sanskrit name of *manipura*) which is your power centre. Focus on drawing the energy from your solar plexus up your body so that it mingles with the energies you have raised through chant and visualisation. This may take a degree of practice. You may need to visualise the two energies as lights extending from you and moving into you to assist with the sensation. Practice is the key when developing any kind of energetic or magical technique.

When you feel that you have achieved your goal, end your rite in your usual manner. Thank the gods and goddesses if you have called upon them, as well as the elemental forces. If you have physically cast a circle, you will need to open or release it. If you need to extinguish the candle, do so using a candle snuffer or the back of a spoon, or even pinching the flame with moistened fingers as opposed to blowing out the flame. It has long been an occult belief that if you blow out a candle flame that you have lit, especially for spell work, then you are effectively extinguishing your magic along with the flame. Your candle is ready to be relit again the following night if you are doing a seven-day spell in which every night for seven consecutive nights (preferably at the same time) you perform the same spell and ritual.

If you wish your candle to burn out, then place it somewhere where it can burn out safely, such as the kitchen sink, where it will not be knocked over.

When it comes to burning a candle for a seven-day spell or something similar, some people mark the candle to ensure that it burns to a certain point each time they light it. If this is not possible, ensure that your candle has completely burned down before the end of the moon circle to result in a positive outcome.

In the United States, novena candles can be easily purchased and used for seven-day candle spells. These candles come in glass cylinder jars, often with specific images stuck to the glass. Where I live in Australia, these candles are difficult to come by, save from ordering online from international companies. The closest type of candle I have been able to find can be purchased from Catholic supply shops. These, however, tend to come in red plastic containers instead of glass. I personally detest having plastic on my altar or using it within my magical workings, so I simply use a pillar candle that I have marked into seven equal sections with an inscribing tool (i.e. toothpick or knife).

Prayer to the Waxing Moon

Hail, Lady Lunar, beautiful jewel of the sky
You grow upon each rising, how fortunate am I
To witness your increasing beauty, bestow your blessings upon me
Hail to you, Lady Lunar, the night-time goddess that I see.

Magical Waxing Crescent Moon Workings

Use this time to perform waxing, drawing, increasing or growth spells. Spells and magical workings include enhancing one's goals and projects, and anything relating to animals, business, change, emotions and matriarchal strength. The waxing crescent moon is a good time for new ventures, initiating new projects and love and health.

Waxing First Quarter Moon

From 6 to 9.5 days after the appearance of the first sliver of the new moon is the time of the first quarter waxing moon. The lunar orb is now from 90° to 135° ahead of the sun and is 50% visible because it is a quarter of the way into its journey around Earth. The moon rises in the middle of the day and sets around midnight. Because the moon is positioned between the sun and Earth, the sunlight side of Earth reflects its light on the night side of the moon lying in shadow.

The deceptive imagery of fragility and hesitancy of the new moon has gone and now the moon is growing rapidly, visible for not only a good portion of the night but into the day as well. As Lady Lunar increases and becomes more solid in shape, so too do any initial visions that we have created at the new moon. Each night, the moon becomes more prominent, inching closer to fullness. In doing so, it has passed the milestone of uncertainty, ensuring us that strength and momentum abounds. As we reflect the moon, we too may be shining brighter and be full of confidence, yet there is still a way to go before our goals and desires are truly manifested. Additional changes may surface, making the journey noticeable and stimulating as our personal efforts begin to show and become noticed by others.

Any glitches or challenges experienced during the waxing crescent phase may have made way for more challenges. However, as we can begin to observe some real effects taking place, this gives us something solid to fight for.

Any stresses of development that have come to light during the waxing crescent moon phase have now passed and been put into motion as the momentum continues to grow with the moon. A feeling of success and achievement is evident. However, it is important not to give up just yet, especially because the goal has not been reached. It is simple to ease up on the work and personal development, thinking that things are going well and that the goal is within reach. However, any lack of attention or desire to rest on our laurels at this critical stage could result in us missing the goal at the most critical time. Therefore, now is the time to take deliberate action, to remain focused on our goals, to make decisions as our self-confidence and self-esteem increases. It is also the time to make decisive and assertive approaches to ensure that we are able to completely harness the energy that this first quarter moon offers in order to truly move forward. As the saying goes, the show is not over until the fat lady sings, and the fat lady, Lady Lunar, is not singing quite yet.

Independence and individuality are important reminders around this time, especially as everyone around us will be feeling the same lunar energy. This may result in people feeling confident and assertive; therefore, it is a timely reminder to avoid conflicts whenever possible and learn to compromise. While we may not want other people interfering in the progress of our goals and desires, it is also important for us not to interfere in theirs.

As inspirations have now taken shape and are moving from vagueness to reality while the momentum gathers, visions are now coming to the attention of others. Excitement and enthusiasm are returning as our hard work and dedication begin to pay off. Keep in mind that not all attention received from other people may be positive. A timely reminder, therefore, that not everything needs to be shared until it has actually been brought into manifestation.

During the first quarter, we can take deliberate action to rectify any problems that may have surfaced during the crescent moon phase. Now is an excellent time to plan, structure and make decisions, striving for efficiency and productivity. It is easy to develop confidence during the first quarter, meaning that now is a good time to work on self-esteem issues and lack of confidence.

It is also a good time to tackle difficult or challenging projects, to commence health or exercise programs, to organise remedial, changing routines and to do whatever is needed to move in the right direction.

Things may be happening faster than you realise. You need to remain focused and be quick to act. There is a great deal of energy around for you to tap into as the moon increases, moving closer and closer to its fullness. Avoid conflicts whenever possible, try to compromise, yet do not allow yourself to become a doormat. Independence and individuality are important elements during this phase of the moon. This applies to others around you as well – do not interfere in the progress of other people, just as you would not allow them to interfere in your own progress.

The first quarter moon can sometimes be referred to as 'crisis in action', reflecting on the need or push to continue moving forward. The vision created at the new moon that faced the stresses of development at the crescent moon is now ready to be put into action. This forward movement, however, requires you to continually build momentum and take action. The best way to do this is to refine the plan and act upon it. The key is to know where you are going and how you will arrive there. It is important, therefore, to make the most of this momentum;

otherwise, you may find yourself running blindly as the energy propels you forward.

First Quarter Moon Journal Exercise

At this stage in the lunar manifestation cycle, some doubts about your ability to manifest your goals and dreams may be setting in. You may wish to commence by drawing a quarter moon in your journal. Anytime that you find this happening, refer back to your manifestation list or vision board that was created with the new moon, and ask yourself:

- Do these goals and dreams still apply?
- Do they still hold the same meaning and purpose for me?

The first quarter moon reminds us that we need to have commitment to achieve something and resolve if we realise that we no longer desire something or someone in our lives. Listen to your heart and gut. Read the list that you have constructed again. What reactions do you notice when you read the list again? You will know in your heart and gut if a desire that you have written down is still something that you are after. If you find yourself uninterested in a dream, now is the time to let it go. It is not worth the energy at this time anyhow. Refocus your energy into working towards manifesting those things that you are passionate about.

You may feel the need to make a new list, a new collage or even re-image achieving your new dreams. If this occurs, it is perfectly fine. This stage in the process can be likened to weeding out the unwanted seedlings in order for the more important ones to grow stronger.

Also, take note of any issues that may arise during this time. Are there any particular instances that are making you work harder to achieve your goals and dreams? If so, this may be because the moon is 'squared' (at a hard 90° angle) to the sun. In astrology, when the moon is in this relationship to the sun, it is common for something to arise that needs to be addressed; some action needs to be taken. Some other points to consider during this phase of the moon are:

- What makes you unique?
- What sets you apart from everyone else?

Write in your journal the qualities you love about yourself and what you hope to realise.

Prayer for the First Quarter Moon

Hail, Lady Lunar, Goddess of the half-light
You move between the spaces of dark and light
Bestow your blessings down upon me
As I honour you, Lady Lunar, so mote it be.

Magical Waxing First Quarter Moon Workings

Now is the time to put on a little extra power to things and push forward towards manifestation, and focus on success, health and partnerships. Magical workings include developing courage, elemental magic, friendships, luck and motivation.

Waxing Gibbous Moon

From 10 to 13.5 days after the new moon, Lady Lunar increases from being 51% to being 99% visible in the night's sky. Her silvery orb is 135° to 180° ahead of the sun because she has moved into the waxing gibbous phase of her journey. The waxing gibbous moon rises between noon and sunset and sets after midnight, rising in the east while the sun is setting in the west. Being far from the sun, the moon is no longer hidden by the sun's glare. The word 'gibbous' comes from the root word meaning 'humpback' or 'bulging'. Therefore, the gibbous waxing moon may seem as if it is bulging with potential, almost appearing full.

Being far from the sun, Lady Lunar has well and truly stepped out from its glare, and therefore, she appears brilliant and nearly round, illuminating the darkness of night. This is truly a breathtaking sight. We might have to glance at her twice, or even consult an astrological calendar, as we approach the end of the gibbous phase. Her energy is strong as we gaze at the silvery disc overhead. She is nearly but not quite as poised as she seems, hesitating. It is almost as if she is taking a deep breath before her big night. With time and patience, Lady Lunar proceeds along her path. It will come, but not yet.

We too seem poised and ready; we can almost touch the goal that we have been manifesting. Almost, yet something is stopping us. Things are not quite coming together as they should. Maybe there is one more detail or an element that is lacking. Maybe we do not feel 100% prepared or have encountered a last-minute glitch. Do we give up, after working this long and hard, after pouring so much energy into our project during the first quarter phase? If we are following the example that Lady Lunar has been showing us, flowing with her energy, then we continue, for we know that our goal will be reached – things will occur. Our dreams will manifest soon.

The waxing gibbous phase holds a great deal of power and potential. It may take some patience and determination to tap into it. We find ourselves at the precarious point of being very close to a goal only to have something else arise. This, however, is not a bad thing. This phase of the moon is all about refining, fine-tuning and tuning in. What we have begun may seem ready, but it can be better. Challenges, really, are always opportunities in disguise. This is truer than ever during the gibbous phase. When you find yourself encountering glitches in your plans, realise that it is fortunate you discovered them at this stage, and most likely the result will be improving and enriching your endeavours.

Patience is the key during this phase of the moon, yet it is not a passive patience. We are not able to simply sit there quietly and wait. We are called to ensure that things are done right. We need to analyse, refine, strengthen and perfect. We need to take on board any constructive criticism that we may have received, drawing inspiration and guidance from Lady Lunar, who is taking her time, developing the perfect form to create a spectacular display when the moment has come, and not before.

The moon's waxing gibbous phase is a good time to revive what has been let slide. If you have (good) habits and routines you have strayed from, it is now time to work on reclaiming them. Do you need to enhance any of your skills and knowledge?

Though we have nearly reached the full moon, the light is still increasing, and we are still in the waxing, growing portion of the cycle. It is still an appropriate time to start a project or launch something new. Unless you want to encounter the resistance of trying to promote growth in something with ingrained diminishing tendencies, this is your last chance (or you can wait a couple of weeks before the next cycle). Therefore, often the kinds of things we begin during this phase are those we have been procrastinating on, rather than things that were planned and targeted for launching in this phase. If you do not want new beginnings during the waning moon and have not yet started them, it is now or never. Not really never, but you will have to wait a couple of weeks.

We tend to easily avoid acting and to procrastinate, but if we are running out of time, we suddenly become ready and impatient. You can call it synchronicity; you did not plan it this way, yet this kind of energy fits well with the gibbous phase. Because the full moon is so very near, a feeling of impatience is in the air. Because so many things are almost complete, but not quite ready, there is a natural rush of sorts. So, if you find yourself frantically scrambling to launch something that you had not yet begun and suddenly cannot wait for, do not feel that you have become out of tune. However, do inject some logic before you become carried away. Ask yourself a few questions:

- Can it wait until the next cycle?
- If so, are you actually ready; how much could it benefit from more preparation time?

Like the other phases, the waxing gibbous phase will bring its own unique energy and inclination to begin things now (whether this is when you planned the launch or it was a last-minute impulse). Things begun during the gibbous phase are likely to need refining and fine-tuning. There is a tendency to perpetually seek improvement. This is a good time to launch things that are only a rough idea; the refining, perfecting and tweaking will come quite naturally. It is also a good time to begin generally analytical or highly detail-orientated projects.

Prosperity Manifestation

During the waxing phases of the moon, it is common for people to want to focus on increasing prosperity. Have you ever taken the time out to consider what 'prosperity' actually means to you? The dictionary meaning is that it is the condition of being successful or thriving, especially in a more economic sense. However, there is so much more to the concept of 'prosperity' than simply money. Will the abundance of money truly improve your life or are there other areas in your life that need 'prosperity' and that will have a wide-reaching effect of abundance?

Any prosperity ritual will depend on the area in your life that you wish to focus on. In many magical traditions, the colour associated with prosperity is green, as in the 'greenback' (the US dollar). However, you can also draw on the energy of Jupiter for expanding business, for example.

Within Chinese cultures, one lucky charm is the Maneki Neko, or Lucky Money Cat, which usually comes in the form of a seated cat with a raised and beckoning front paw that waves. You may have seen this cat in Asian shops. It is believed that these cats call in wealth and prosperity to the home or business. Further, as cats are able to see in the dark, the lucky cats also frighten away evil spirits that may hamper success.

A simple prosperity manifestation spell is to half fill a bowl with water and place a silver coin in it. Position the bowl where the light of the approaching full moon can shine into the water. Gently sweep your hands above the surface, symbolically gathering up the moon's rays. As you do this, recite the following chant three times:

> Lady Lunar, beautiful moon,
> Bring your wealth to me real soon.
> Fill my hands with silver and gold.
> All you give, my hands can hold.

When you have finished, you can pour the water onto the ground and bury the coin in the earth. Alternatively place the coin in the next charity tin that you see to spread the abundance.

Prayer to the Gibbous Moon

> Hail Lady Lunar, She of beaming silver
> Your growing abundance sends darkness aquiver
> Shining bright amongst the stars you rise high
> Hail to your Lady Lunar, Goddess of the night's sky.

Magical Waxing Gibbous Moon Workings

This is the time to catch loose ends or make necessary changes. Magical workings include drawing, increasing or growth.

The Full Moon

How sweet the moonlight sleeps upon this bank!
Here will we sit, and let the sounds of music
Creep in your ears: soft stillness, and the night,
Become the touches of sweet harmony.
Sit, Jessica: look, how the floor of heaven
Is thick inlaid with patines of bright gold:
There's not the smallest orb which thou behold'st,
But in his motion like an angel sings,
Still quiring to the young-ey'd cherubims.
('The Merchant of Venice' by William Shakespeare)

It is now 14 days after the new moon and the lunar orb is exactly opposite the sun. Because she is positioned behind Earth, Lady Lunar's whole surface is lit by the sun as she rises at sunset and sets at dawn. With the sun and the moon on either side of Earth, it is as if Earth is the fulcrum of a seesaw – when the sun sets in the west, the full moon rises, and when the sun rises again in the east, the full moon sets.

As Lady Lunar is reaching the peak of her cycle, and even though during the evening of the full moon she is shining in all her brilliant glory, it is a great time for rejuvenation and to refine any intentions because we are now able to connect with our visions. We feel her energies as they heighten our intuitive abilities, our psychic awareness and our ability to obtain enlightenment. If we gaze upwards, her lunar glow illuminates the darkness, making the shadows seem alive and vibrant. As the sun illuminates the moon, the moon transforms and reflects this light upon Earth. The illuminated Earth transforms and reflects the moonlight back, producing a somewhat mystical, silvery glow. These energies of illumination and reflection are ingrained into the phase of the full moon. We reflect upon our lives and selves; we see more deeply into our own souls as well as those of others. We are drawn to the illusive and mysterious.

The full moon is considered one of the most powerful and influential times within the whole lunar cycle. There is an out-of-control tendency that can make it difficult to harness this energy. The best advice is to use your self-awareness. To ride the emotional tides that the full moon pulls upon, it is best to be aware of or in touch with your emotions. If you approach the full moon feeling as if your life is spinning out of control, there is a strong possibility that it simply might just be doing that. One solution is to surrender to the emotional waves until the waxing moon appears and then focus on being more open to learning, spiritual growth and even bringing some structure into your life.

We may be only halfway through the lunar cycle, yet there is a feeling of culmination. It is almost as if what we have been steadily working towards during the waxing moon has finally all come together and manifested into our goal. Cast your mind back to your vision board or the list that you made at the new moon. How many of these things have come to fruition because you have put the effort into them? If your goal has not been realised, the light of the full moon will illuminate where you have miscalculated. Preparation and the right mind frame are key to the successful, productive use of this notorious moon phase.

While the energy of the full moon is often said to last for three days – the day before, the day of and the day just after the actual date – my preference is to undertake any full moon rite on the eve, just before the actual date. This ensures that if I am working with the lunar energies, I have captured them as close to the peak as I can before they begin to wane again. To find the exact timing of the full moon, I use the website timeanddate.com because it calculates anomalies, such as daylight savings. Other sites that I refer to can be found in the Resources section at the end of this book.

The energy of each full moon is different as the moon moves

through the different astrological signs (which I mention in Part II). Becoming aware of these different astrological keys enables us to notice any shifts that may be occurring at a deeper and often more subtle level in our lives. At her peak, Lady Lunar is all about change. Therefore, while the full moon energies are often associated with manifestation, I tend to enable this through the progress of releasing and purging what has hindered me from obtaining my goals.

Full Moon Ritual of Release

There are many ways to use the illuminating effect of the full moon. Astrologer Yasmine Boland[12] suggests using most of the full moon energy to forgive someone who may have done you wrong, even when you may have perceived their actions as wronging you. She advises that when we are upset or angry with a person, our own emotion locks us into that particular point in time. Therefore, it is easy for us to feed off this energy, which only causes the spiral of pain or anger to increase and the energy to become darker and heavier. Through the act of forgiveness, our energy becomes lighter as we lessen our emotional attachment.

I really like this idea. Too often, even if we think that we have forgiven someone, on a deeper level we are still holding on to the feeling of being hurt or angry, disappointed or let down by that person. We may even feel that to forgive means to forget, when, in fact, these are two completely different things. When we forgive, we lessen our emotional attachment to the incident and sometimes even to the person, allowing us to move on. Forgiveness only truly works, however, when we are ready to forgive completely and mean it at all energetic levels of our being.

To use the full moon energy to release outdated and prohibiting emotional attachments, begin with taking a couple of deep breaths to calm yourself. When you are settled, think of an incident, habit, thought pattern, idea or upset you wish to release and write it down. If there is a person involved, write their name down along with what they did or what you did to them. The incident does not need to be recent; it could be something that occurred a number of years ago that you are still holding on to for some reason. If you have more than one person or incident, that is fine. You are creating a 'forgiveness list' that you can use to release outdated emotional attachments.

When you have constructed your list, close your eyes and visualise one situation or person. As you focus on this image, visualise it being surrounded by a bubble. Boland suggests a 'bubble of pink unconditional love'. However, if you are not able to do this, a clear bubble is perfectly fine.

As you hold this visualisation, state the following, and as you do, see the person or incident in the bubble disappearing or floating away:

Lady Lunar, round and full
Allow me to forgive those who have caused me ill
All past experiences and memories
My own mistakes take from me
May there be peace where anger stood
Surrounded by unconditional love
Lady Lunar release all from me
And bestow forgiveness, so mote it be.

Check in with your feelings. How do you feel about this person or incident? If you still feel some emotions, you might want to repeat this section before moving on to the next person or incident on your list. If you feel no emotional attachment at all, you may like to chant 'May you be happy, may you be free' a couple of times as a way of cementing your release. This wording comes from a Buddhist Tonglen practice that is based on releasing emotional attachments through forgiveness.

Alternatively, you could visualise an emotional energetic cord connecting you and this person. When you recite the chant, visualise the cord dissolving. If the person is to remain in your life, however, a fresh cord can be established that does not contain the negative emotional residue from the past.

You can release and forgive as many or as few people or incidents on your list as you feel capable of doing in any one sitting. If you have released all from your list, burn it and dispose of the ashes either in a rubbish bin at the crossroads (where two or more roads or streets meet) or, as I do, bury them in your garden.

Purging Full Moon Ritual

Another use of the full moon energy is to purge or remove something from your life. To do this, write down on separate pieces of paper the things that you want to release or change. These pieces of paper are often called 'petitions'. You may wish to make a small fire, or simply use a candle. Ensure that you also have a fireproof container handy.

- Cleanse and make sacred the area you are using in a manner that resonates with you. You might like to use white sage, pine needles, frankincense or an incense stick, say an opening prayer or affirmation, or undertake a proper circle casting, such as the one that I have provided in the New Moon section in Part V of this book.
- When you are ready, light your candle. If you are outside, look skyward to see if you can witness the moon. If not, or if you are inside, close your eyes and image the full moon directly overhead.
- Take a couple of deep breaths into your diaphragm, centring and grounding yourself as you connect to the moment and what you are about to do. Then, one by one, read aloud the words you have written on each piece of paper. As you vocalise what you want to release or change in your life, you are setting your intention to

release that item, attitude or even addiction from your life. Once you have spoken the words, carefully hold the paper in the fire or candle flame that it ignites and once caught, quickly drop the paper into the fireproof container.

- Once you have released something from your life, it is a good idea to fill that gap, so to speak, with something, even if it is inner peace, or clarity in readiness for any manifestation work yet to be undertaken.
- The ashes from your petitions are to be disposed of as above.

Expressing Gratitude

If the previous two uses of the full moon energy do not appeal to you, maybe you feel the need to simply sit in the lunar light and be grateful for all that has been illuminated. Sometimes the full moon enables us to see those normally invisible, dark aspects of our own personality, the parts that we keep hidden in the shadows, out of view. We all have these parts. Within Jungian-based psychology, they are called our 'shadow self', and in other teachings they are known as 'inner child'. You might like to use this time to take a closer look at what is in your shadow to see whether there is hidden potential or opportunities that may have been overlooked.

Expressing gratitude during the full moon, even for the mistakes I have made, is a practice I personally do. I acknowledge what I have received and achieved over the waxing lunar cycle, including the challenges, and allow that inner knowledge to format into what is needed to be released during the waning cycle.

Focus on gratitude for what you have in the here and now rather than on what you long for, which can lead to resentment and misery, or even anger. Gratitude is often a forgotten quality in this modern commercially driven world, where we focus on our 'first-world' problems instead of the simpler things that really matter in life. Our social media feeds are filled with images of what other people allegedly have, which can make us feel less worthy. So, being able to express gratitude for things that we have in our own lives can attract a higher energetic vibration, which in turn assists us when we are feeling at our lowest. The expression of gratitude also acts as a timely reminder of what is actually important.

Think of three things that you are truly grateful for: people, instances, feelings and so on, and write them down. Focus on each item (or person) that you are grateful for and what it means to you. Then express the reasons out loud three times. For example:

- 'I am grateful for [item] because it brings me peace.'
- 'I am grateful for [item] because it makes me whole.'
- 'I am grateful for [person] because they show me unconditional love.'
- 'I am grateful for [person] because the challenges they present to me enable me to grow as a spiritual being.'

As mentioned above, focusing on why something or someone is important to us can assist us when faced with social media feeds of what appears to be perfection, yet often is at a very superficial level only.

You may like to burn your list afterwards or write it in your magical diary or journal. You might also like to keep a special page, say at the back of your diary/journal, to record your gratitude list so that you can refer to it during the times when you are feeling sad or disappointed with the world.

Full Moon Anointing Oil

Another thing that I personally do when I want to connect with the full moon on a deeper level is to anoint myself with an appropriately blended oil. I include some blends in Part III of this book; however, the following is another recipe you might like to make just prior to the full moon that you can use to anoint your pulse points, such as the wrists and inner elbow.

Measure 10 ml of a carrier oil (such as jojoba or extra virgin olive oil) into a clean glass jar. Mix together 13 drops of sandalwood essential oil, three drops of jasmine essential oil and one drop of rose essential oil. Once it is blended, you can further decant the oil into a bottle if you do not want to keep it in the jar.

Rose (*Rosa damascene*) essential oil is one of the most expensive and most adulterated essential oils in aromatherapy practice. This is because it is difficult to extract and takes several thousand rose petals to produce a minute quantity of oil. An alternative for rose essential oil is geranium (*Pelargonium graveolens*). Do not, however, be tempted to substitute an essential oil for a 'fragrant' oil, which is an artificial oil devoid of any magical or medicinal properties.

Making and Charging Moon Water

Technically, all water has been infused by the moon. If social media is anything to go by, it would seem that water put out under the rays of the full moon will be imbued with magical lunar powers; the water can then be used to cleanse your altar or sacred space, or crystals, or to be added to bathwater or even drunk. I guess, in some way, this is true. However, it depends on what intent has been instilled into the water. In 2004, Japanese bestselling author Masaru Emoto indicated that human consciousness can affect the molecular structure of water.[13] Therefore, in effect, any water can be 'charged', regardless of whether it is placed under the moon's rays or not.

Having said that, an old-fashioned way of creating moon water that has been handed down to me is to make a potion that consists of not only water that has been charged with the moon but also a corresponding herb or a selection of herbs for a specific purpose. To create moon water this way, you will need to use a glass jar that can be secured with a lid, both of which are thoroughly purified, washed and sterilised. I sterilise my jars by placing them freshly washed in an oven that has been preheated to 160–180° C (320–385° F) for about 15 minutes.

Fill the jar with one cup of spring or filtered water and place within the water a small piece of dried gingerroot (*Zingiber officinale*), half teaspoon of dried chamomile (*Chamaemelum nobis*) or a sprig of rosemary (*Rosmarinaus officinalis*).

Seal the lid tightly on the jar. Allow the jar and its contents to bathe in the glow of the moon for one night. Check a lunar calendar for the correct date for the particular phase of the moon you want as well as the astrological sign. Another point I would make is that if you are adding botanicals to water, keep in mind that over time they will decompose. Therefore, it is probably much safer to make smaller batches of moon water each lunar cycle. Any leftover water can be used to water plants and be given back to the earth.

Some old spells call for the moon water to be made with mandrake root (*Mandragora officinarum*). Mandrake does have powerful lunar connections; however, not only is this root often difficult to come by (especially where I live in Australia), it is also poisonous. Therefore, it should never be used in anything that is going to be ingested. I mention more about moon water in Part II when I talk about drawing down the moon.

Prayer to the Full Moon

Hail, O Lady Lunar, Queen of full light
Your chariot shines brightly at night
Look down, Lady Lunar, as I honour thee
For all the blessings you have bestowed upon me.

Magical Full Moon Workings

Magical workings for full moon focus on prophecy, protection, healing and celebration. Magical workings include love and romance, artistic endeavours, knowledge, self-improvement, self-empowerment, families, legal undertakings and psychic matters.

The Waning Moons
(Disseminating, Last Quarter, Waning)

And like a dying lady, lean and pale,
Who totters forth, wrapp'd in a gauzy veil,
Out of her chamber, led by the insane
And feeble wanderings of her fading brain,
The moon arose up in the murky East,
A white and shapeless mass.
('The Waning Moon' by Percy Bysshe Shelley)

Once the moon has reached its peak, Lady Lunar begins to slowly but steadily decrease in size each night, rising from an hour to several hours behind the sun. There are three phases of the waning moon, just as there are three phases of the waxing moon. The first is the disseminating or waning gibbous moon (from 3.5 to 6 days after the full moon), the last quarter (from 6 to 9.5 days from the full moon), and finally the balsamic or waning gibbous (from 10 to 13.5 days from the full moon).

When the moon begins to disappear, it favours completion, letting go and finishing things. During the waning phase of the moon, it is not recommended to commence any new projects. Instead, it is more of a favourable time to remove negativity, overcome addictions, end bad habits or even end emotional situations, including divorce proceedings, stress and anxiety. If you do begin new projects, you may find it difficult to follow through until the new lunar cycle commences again. Instead, try to focus your energy on clearing away unfinished business that will enable you to take full advantage of the new opportunities when they come your way.

Working with the waning phases of the moon can also help you connect with your own inner wisdom as you switch from exerting your energy externally to using it more internally. If you are new to this, you might like to begin by honouring your existence. Too often, our busy modern lives can have us rushing about so that we barely take any notice of what surrounds us on a daily basis. Now that the activity of the new and waxing moon is subsiding, we can do just that. Slow down and stop, if even only for a moment. Allow yourself to become aware of the scents around you – the plants, animals and bird life. Savour the foods that you eat and pay more attention to the daydreams that fill your idle time. When you allow yourself to slow down, even just a little bit, you are granting yourself time to live your life in more than just the physical dimension. Now is the time to ask yourself:

- What do you see when you look past the ordinary?
- Do you experience difference between completion and ending?
- What kinds of dreams are you having? Are you remembering them when you wake?

As the moon turns inward to become square again with the sun, this is the end of the cycle and is a good time to complete or eliminate anything that is no longer necessary. It is a time to mentally clean house. Unwanted habits and other negative influences should be cast away at this time. Some bad habits, such as smoking, can be extremely difficult to break, so it is best to set a realistic time frame. Utilise this time for banishing or manifesting to rid unwanted or stuck energy.

It is also a good time to share the accomplishments of the preceding waxing moon, to reap what we have sown as well as weed and prune what we do not need to clear the way for the new energy.

Disseminating Moon
From three to seven days after the full moon, the moon begins to disappear in the night's sky, until it is only 50% visible and

moves from 135° to 90° behind the sun. The disseminating (also known as the waning gibbous) moon rises mid-evening, almost eerily some hours after sunset, glowing red like the full moon when it is near the horizon. It then sets at mid-morning.

Lady Lunar can look like some kind of a misshapen clone of a full moon when she begins to wane. Even though the full moon phase has passed, she is still able to light up the night sky. As she appears to exhale and let go of her light, we too are encouraged to exhale and let go of all those things we have been holding on to that are no longer of benefit or suitable for us.

It is a time to exhale and take a bit more notice of our surroundings and our place within them. We have, after all, made the transition from waxing to waning, and now it is time to see what is waiting for us. The disseminating phase is integrative. Our awareness of others – their needs and goals, and their effect on us – is heightening. We begin to see where our knowledge may be useful to others and how their knowledge may be of use to us. The vision that began at the new moon, the fulfilment gained at the full moon and the experiences in between have all begun transforming into wisdom and understanding. We become more receptive to absorbing the energy and knowledge of other people just as we also feel more compelled to share what we have learned with others.

Communication is vital during the disseminating phase of the moon. It is only the start of the waning half of the lunar cycle after all and so we are only beginning to seek a deeper level of understanding. At the full moon, things are fully illuminated and accomplished as our goals are reached and ideas are solidified. Now we know. But do we understand? Our mind has been busy, gathering and sharing information, racing with the many thoughts that have been revealed. Now is the time to stop and begin to process those thoughts, bits of information, experiences and even memories that have come our way. As we process them, we transform them into wisdom and a much needed valuable tool that we can use for the rest of the waning lunar cycle, and what follows from that.

Sharing information is one of the critical elements of the disseminating lunar phase. If you have a message to communicate, now is the time. If other people are talking, especially if it is about something relevant, listen to what they are saying. Give them your full attention. Now is the time to focus on study, learning and absorbing ideas and information. The tendency to share and interact is not limited to information, although that is its primary influence. This can be an excellent time to socialise, teach children to share or undertake charity work. Is there a class at your local community or adult education centre that you are interested in attending, or a workshop that you maybe could teach that will be of assistance to other people? You might even find yourself making friends with people who you connect with on an intellectual level. Keep an open mind to the array of possibilities and opportunities that could be coming your way.

The disseminating lunar phase can be a busy time, at least mentally. However, in the rush to share and learn new ideas, keep in mind that the general tendency of the waning moon is one of decreasing and letting go. As such, it is a good time to break habits, release outdated perceptions, change routines and weed out ideas that are not useful. Be open to change because this phase is the beginning of a transformation. Ask yourself:

- What do I feel is holding me back from achieving my goals?
- What do I need to change?
- What can I change that will help me achieve a more peaceful life?

Lady Lunar's disseminating phase also marks the beginning of transformation and change. Even in things we want to progress and grow in, the balance of waning is essential. Do you have a stalled project or feel stuck in a rut? Then something has to change for new doors to open and new opportunities to be received. Too often people look externally when it comes to change, as if believing that the responsibility lies with other people. The truth, however, is that the only person who completely rules our life is our own self. If something needs to be removed to make room for new and better opportunities, there are times when we simply have to do the hard work and finally let go of and release those old beliefs, possessions and relationships that are no longer working.

Moon Mirror Healing

During the disseminating phase of the moon, you may wish to help a person by offering them some distant healing.

Begin by placing a silver mirror face up on your altar or a sacred space so that the light of the waning moon shines upon it. In the centre of the mirror, place a symbol to represent the person who the healing is for. This symbol could be a photo, a piece of jewellery or lock of hair, or a name on a business card. If you have none of these items, then you can always simply write their name on a piece of paper.

Use the symbol on the mirror in the moonlight as a focal point as you visualise that the one needing healing is becoming well and then is healthy. After the ritual, deliver the symbol to the subject of the healing rite as an additional way of transmitting healing.

Cleanse the mirror you used by passing it through the smoke of white sage (*Salvia apiana*), frankincense, cedar, copal, dammar or any other incense that has purification properties. Then your mirror will be ready for you to use for other healing work in the future. I also use a spray that I make specifically for cleansing sacred objects that I use in ritual or other magical workings, and which I sell through my LunaNoire Creations Etsy store.

Disseminating Moon Ritual

As the moon continues to wane, it offers the opportunity for us to begin going within, to finalise loose ends and to sit and reflect on where our journey has taken us so far. Are you heading in the direction you want to be heading in? If not, what is preventing you from realistically achieving what your soul desires? As the evening sky grows darker with each passing night, it almost invites you to focus on your own inner light – your soul spark – and to provide it with the nurturance it needs.

- Prepare your sacred space in the manner you feel comfortable undertaking, or you may like to use the ritual format mentioned in the New Moon section or contained in Part V of this book. You will also need a fireproof container and some paper to write your petitions on, which you will then burn. If you work with crystals, you may also like to have with you a piece of lapis lazuli (to help with reflection and clarity), angelite (to restore tranquillity), lepidolite (to eliminate stress and anxiety) or any other appropriate crystals that you are drawn to.

- Settle yourself before your lit candle, take a couple of deep breaths into your diaphragm. As you inhale, visualise that you are breathing in the calming and healing lunar energies from the moon. As you exhale, visualise that you are releasing stress, tension and anxiety from your body. Even though you may not feel anxious, it almost natural for your body to tend to hold these feelings in ways that can often go unnoticed.

- When you feel relaxed and focused, turn your attention to what you have learned over the past few weeks. If you have your lunar journal handy, you might like to reflect back and see what messages or instances have kept arising. Are there any signs as to what is holding you back?

- Since the disseminating moon is a good time to focus on releasing things from your life, be it illness, negative people, or emotions you may want to help overcome, write some of these down on pieces of paper. Before you burn the pieces of paper, bring to mind what you would like them to be replaced with.

- For example, if you wish to remove an illness, you may wish to replace it with good health; to release anger, you may want to replace it with calmness or peace.

- As you burn each negative trait, you may like to recite a statement or chant such as the following:

Lady Lunar, with your fading light
Take from me my negative sight
Bestow upon me peace and calm
As you bless me and this charm.

- Hold your chosen crystal and as you do, visualise the change having occurred in your life. This crystal then can be used as a touchstone that you carry with you throughout the remaining portion of the lunar cycle. Anytime that you feel the old habits creeping back into your life, pause and focus on the crystal; it will act as a reminder of the change you are seeking.

Prayer for the Disseminating Moon

Hail, O Lady Lunar, of the fading light
Ease my troubles as you decrease each night
Exalted Lady, may my problems wane
As my life is blessed in your name.

Magical Disseminating Moon Workings

During this phase of the moon, focus on commencing waning, repelling, decreasing or reversing spells, and removing negativity. Magical workings include overcoming addictions, ending bad habits and ending emotional situations, such as divorce proceedings, stress and anxiety.

Last Quarter Moon

When Lady Lunar appears to be half illuminated again, she has journeyed three-quarters of the way through her orbit around Earth. If we have been paying attention, we will notice that she is facing the other direction in her illumination before she slowly slips into darkness. Each night, we see less and less of her as the shadows grow stronger. Still, however, she shines, showing us the way through the transformation and evolution.

If we reside in the Northern Hemisphere, the darkness is encroaching from the right, while for us south of the equator, it is from the left. She rises around midnight and appears at her highest point in the sky at dawn, before setting around noon. The moon is 90° behind the sun, and at right angles to a line between Earth and the sun.

As the lunar energy wanes, a restless energy may abound as we instinctively feel that something is happening – that change is afoot. We have reached another rather auspicious moment within the lunar cycle with it being half light and half dark, offering us the opportunity to pause and reflect back on where we have come from and then forward in the direction in which we are heading. Darkness is slowly yet steadily taking over the light, drawing us inward, into the quiet, the internal, the mysteries of the shadows, encouraging us to slow down and let go. After the external, extraverted and illuminating energy of the waxing and full moon, the energy of the darkness can feel rather unsettling owing to its powerful deepness.

Cast your mind back over your lunar journal workings, back

to the vision board or list that you created at the new moon.

- Look back: where have you been and what have you done?
- Look ahead: where are you going, and what will you do?

The waning last quarter moon is a time of change. To form plans for the future, the repercussions of the past need to be released, and we need to decide what we will (or must) do to reach our goal. This is not a time to avoid responsibility and make those hard decisions. Because it is a time of balance, we may find ourselves receiving credit for what we have achieved to date, as well as being faced with mistakes we made. Now is the time to use the waning lunar energy to take an honest look at projects or things in our lives that do not seem to be working out and decide whether they are truly worth pursuing. There is a difference between giving up out of frustration and annoyance at not getting what you desire and deciding something is not worth following through after applying a degree of logical thinking. If you are ending the plan, but the goal is still worth striving for, consider a new start – a different approach – in the coming lunar cycle.

Similar to the first quarter moon, the last quarter offers a time of balance that is followed by direction; the difference is now that the energies are encouraging us to release and let go. Therefore, the last quarter moon is an appropriate time to break bad or stubborn habits and to change routines. We may experience a vague feeling of chaos and even conflict in our lives around this time. Be careful not to let things spin out of control. If they do, try not to be too concerned. Breathe and surrender to the process, for this is natural. We are at a turning point after all. There is a delicate balance between releasing control and handing over all responsibility. Try not to let yourself slip into bad habits and not do what has to be done; however, do not push yourself too hard either. Rest and contemplation are integral to the entire waning phase.

The last quarter lunar phase is a good time to take care of details and finalise projects that you have been putting off. Clean out your wardrobe, finish up some paperwork, organise and finally deal with some of those items that you have been neglecting. What needs to be eliminated or weeded out, or even changed? Now is the time to restructuring and reconsider plans. Take a serious look at what has and has not worked, using the information and insight that you have gathered along the way. Now is a good time to focus on finishing or beginning the final stage of something. If you have a project near completion, it can be a good time to take the necessary steps to finish it; make time and room for something new.

Last Quarter Moon Journal Exercise

This is a time of focusing energy on the task at hand. If we try to avoid this, we might find ourselves confronted by others; this can mean that things can begin going 'right' for us with progress made, but it can also mean that things begin going 'wrong' for us – something breaks down on us, people give up on us or give us problems. Things become impossible. Either way, we are now faced with the truth of how we fit into our world, and the outcomes of our acts to date stand before us.

Although we like to think of ourselves as independent, in reality our lives are, to a great degree, in the hands of others. If we have been acting as if we were a victim, we can suffer at this time. What is done is done. The past is beginning to end and a glimmer of the future peeks out at us. At the new moon, the future is reborn as a seed of possibilities for a future cycle.

We all have a role that we have either accepted or rejected and a question pops up before us: What have I received from all of this, and where will it lead me in the end? Draw a waning quarter moon in your journal and ponder or meditate on this question. What thoughts or feelings come to mind?

You might like to also pull a card from an oracle or tarot deck, or any other form of divination to which you are drawn to assist and guide you through this lunar phase. Through the week, some questions you can ask are:

- Where am I at currently?
- What needs to be healed?
- What do I need to let go of?
- What do I need to focus on?

Record your answers in your journal.

Prayer to the Last Quarter Moon

Hail, O Lady Lunar, your balance I see
Half-darkness, half-light, in the sky above me
Goddess of the spaces betwixt and between
Bless me, Lady Lunar, both bright and unseen.

Magical Last Quarter Moon Workings

During this phase of the moon, it is time to release any negativity around us, continue banishing work or support a previous banishing ritual. Magical workings include overcoming addictions, concluding divorce proceedings, protection and banishing ill health and stress.

Waning Balsamic Moon

From 11 to 13.5 days after the full moon, the silver orb is now 45° to nearly 0° behind the sun. It rises at around 3.00am and sets at mid-afternoon so it is not visible in the night sky. This is the time of the balsamic or waning crescent moon, seen in the eastern skies before dawn. Unless we rise early, we often do not see this phase of the moon because as the light of the sun increases, it fades from view. Yet, the waning crescent is there in the sky, nearly all day long, moving ahead of the sun across the sky's dome before it sets in the west several hours or less before sunset.

The moon has nearly completed its orbit of Earth, and is nearly in line with Earth and the sun again. Therefore, the moon is facing mostly away from us again so we only see a slender fraction of the moon's day side – a crescent moon.

The word 'balsamic' comes from *balsam*, meaning 'anything healing or soothing', which, according to Yasmine Boland, is what this last phase of the moon is all about. Our hopes and dreams have become 'explosions of potential: to realisations of what can and cannot be, to acceptance and forgiveness and surrender ... and now comes healing and soothing'.[14]

It is also a time of quiet contemplation as we withdraw more into the inner realms, contemplating and dreaming, feeling and preparing for what may happen next. To a greater degree, we tend to exist within these somewhat 'invisible worlds' of the subconscious, of the spiritual realms and our own inner depths. We are often not consciously aware of what is happening on these inner planes because, externally, it may feel as if nothing much is happening at all. That is, until we stop for a moment and realise that while Lady Lunar releases her current cycle, extinguishing the light and preparing for the next cycle, we are also releasing, extinguishing and preparing, regardless of whether we are consciously aware or not.

We have reached the stage in the lunar cycle, when we can feel an uneasy restlessness. While it is not as chaotic as the last quarter, the energies still seem to stir us, this time on a deeper level. One cycle is ending, yet the new one has not yet begun. It is as if the tides are pushing up against each other, resulting in a void, a sense of emptiness; yet there is a paradox because this moment is filled with everything – the past and the future, our hopes and our fears. Externally, this should be a calm, quiet time. Take a breath and allow yourself opportunity to think, feel and experience. Allow yourself to gain some clarity.

The balsamic moon is about release. The growing and building of the waxing lunar phase has passed; so too has the analysing and changing of the waning phase. Now is the time for acceptance and release. Let things go, especially if they have passed the point of being repairable, and when the lunar cycle commences again, maybe they can be restarted. Through the releasing of what no longer serves us, we open the way for healing to commence, making way, all the while, for something new.

With the new moon approaching, some people view this time of the lunar cycle as one of preparation. As Lady Lunar is retreating into the shadow, withdrawing into herself, resting and preparing to come back strong and vibrant in the next cycle, so too can we. Allow your spirit to be free and your imagination to run wild in readiness for the time when the momentum builds again. Now is the time to return to nature and refresh your spirit. Stop and smell the roses, so to speak. Focus on some mundane tasks that you may automatically undertake without giving them too much thought. If you are able to, avoid strenuous activities, especially those that are mentally strenuous, and allow this time to completely relax with the subtle energies that are ebbing and flowing.

Waning Moon Ritual for Release

Place a bowl of water on the table. Relax. Imagine your image in the bowl of water; allow the brightness of the moon to watch over your reflection. Visualise this for a few minutes. Take your finger and pike it in the water's semi-hard, rippling the water. Say:

Lunar waters, cleanse and waters calm
My mind and heart from this emotional storm.

Repeat this chant over and over again until the water has stopped rippling while visualising yourself within the water being happy and emotionally balanced. Then, empty the water bowl.

Prayer to the Balsamic Moon

Hail, Lady Lunar, crescent jewel in the midnight sky
I am forlorn to see you disappear from high
As you fade, take my troubles from me
Grant me peace, so mote it be.

Magical Balsamic Moon Workings

During this phase of the moon, focus on moving within yourself, to understand your anger and passion, steering them to work in a positive way for you. Magical workings include overcoming addictions, enemies, or quarrels; ending a relationship in a divorce; removing obstacles or physical problems; or stopping stalkers and being a victim of theft.

The Dark Moon

Is the moon tired? She looks so pale
Within her misty veil
She scales the sky form east to west,
And takes no rest.

Before the coming of the night
The moon shows papery white;
Before the dawning of the day
She fades away.
(From "Sing-Song" by Christina Georgina Rossetti)

As mentioned previously, the eight phases of the moon have been accredited to US astrologer Dane Rudhyar. Therefore, it is interesting to note that he never mentioned the dark moon as a lunar phase, calling it instead the new moon. However, from a more esoteric and magical point of view, there is a difference between the two. The dark moon occurs, or refers, to the phase when the moon is not visible at all in the sky. This is for an extremely brief period before the first sliver of light begins to appear again.

With the moon rising around the same time as the sun in the morning and setting at around sunset, for the briefest period, there is no light in the night sky. Therefore, it is the time of ultimate rest, the pause that occurs between the breaths, and the time of deepest silence. Then when we exhale, the light gradually returns again.

When the sky is cloaked in complete darkness, it becomes easier for us to shed unnecessary emotional baggage, and let go of those people and ideas that no longer serve or add value to our lives. It is a time to cleanse our own selves and create space so that what is new can enter. The dark moon pulls us inwards, luring us to look deeper into the longings of our soul. It offers us a much-needed time of rest and reflection, and the opportunity to simply be. For some people, however, the act of simply sitting still can cause agitation, especially if they are used to being on the go all the time. However, it is here within the darkness that powerful dreams can be experienced, we can retrieve past life memories or to delve deeply into our own psyches to see what is presented to us.

The dark moon symbolises two things. The first is the unknowing of what is to come and a reminder that it is okay to feel uncertain during this period of darkness. Therefore, we are encouraged to go within, removing ourselves from the stimulus of the bright outside world. The second aspect of the dark moon is potential – we are being offered a blank canvas to fill with our inspiration. While the sky is moonless, we have the power to create and plant seeds of intention for the coming cycle.

During the briefest time of the dark moon, we can perform manifestations for prophecy, chaos or even cursing. However, as with the ways of magic, if you curse another, then be prepared to reap what you have sown. Society has led us to believe that the colour black is negative or filled with fear. However, instead of being an absence of colour, black encompasses all of the colours. Therefore, it also dispels negativity.

I find that when I am working with the energies of Lady Lunar, I am doing so primarily to focus on improving my own life. Therefore, I have found that the more I allow myself to ebb and flow with her tides, the less the actions of other people affect me. This is because I largely focus on what I need in my life and leave other people to their own devices. In my nearly 30 years of working magic, I have probably had the need to perform only a handful of more baneful spells. Even then, in these circumstances, an element of protection has been involved. After all, there is a hermetic principle found within most esoteric and magical teachings of 'like attracting like'.

If you focus your use of the dark moon energy primarily on cursing, either performing curses or preventing yourself from being cursed, then what you are in effect doing is attracting more and more of this energy into your life. The end result could be the development of a degree of paranoia. The event of someone projecting an effective magical curse at you, on the whole, is a rarity. More often than not, the true cause is within our own self. Instead of projecting outwards in a defensive manner, take a moment to breathe and move inward, taking this opportunity to release and let go, bringing yourself back into alignment with your soul's desire.

Use this brief period that is the dark moon as a time of great introspection to ascertain how to manifest the life that you truly want. Ask yourself the following questions, recording your responses in your lunar journal:

- When the moon was full, I saw unlimited potential. What might be missing?
- What or who no longer serves me, and why?
- What seemingly negative things will I actively choose to see as a positive?

Use this somewhat mysterious time to set the foundation so that you can mould any creative experiences that will manifest over the coming weeks. Rest, recuperate and invite calm and serenity into your world as you delve into reflection on your life. Where do you want to go from here? How can you create the conditions that will replenish your spirit and indulge them fully? What does 'replenish your spirit' mean to you? Does it include reading, journal writing, meditation, artwork or listening to music? Maybe you have one of those friends whose company you can enjoy because they simply allow you to be.

Dark Moon Releasing Ritual

This ritual is different from the one you performed during the balsamic moon in that you are calling forth the aspects of yourself that you want to release from your life. It does require a degree of visualisation and concentration. You will also have to believe in your own magical ability for it to be successful. Therefore, I would recommend that if you undertake the following, you keep your workings to yourself. This will prevent any negativity from non-believers potentially seeding any doubt into your mind.

For this ritual you will need a black candle, a fireproof bowl, some paper and a pen. Black candles are used because they open up the deeper levels of the unconscious mind. They are also good for banishing negativity from your life.

Place the fireproof bowl in the middle of your altar or working space, with the paper and pen next to it. Cast your circle in a widdershins[15] direction. If you are not familiar with this process, refer to the ritual given in the New Moon section. Alternatively, you will find a lunar ritual that can be adapted in the appendix at the end of this book.

Once you cast your circle and return to face your altar, move again to face the south[16] if you are in the Southern Hemisphere, or the north if you are in the Northern Hemisphere. Then light your candle. As you do this, say:

At this time of the month when the moon hides
I honour the Dark Mother from where she resides
O Wise One, Ancient One, listen to my plea.
I call on your wisdom to release these aspects from me.

Visualise the different parts of your life that you are ready to let go of as strongly as you can. As you bring each part into your mind's eye, imagine binding them together with a cord made from divine light and then direct the bound parts into the candle. As you watch these parts being devoured by the flame, visualise them again well and truly leaving your body and your thought process. Take a couple of deep breaths and truly believe that these aspects of you have been completely dissolved.

When you have finished, close your eyes and focus on allowing any 'gaps' that these removed parts may have caused being filled with healing energy. Take another deep breath, move widdershins to the east and say:

O Dark Mother, Ancient One, of the midnight skies
I thank you for aiding me in healing my life
Release, renew, and set myself free.
As my will, so mote it be.

If you want to sit and meditate, allowing your energetic field to realign, then use this time to do just that. If you have cast a circle at the beginning of your ritual, you will need to call it back. Some people call back circles by walking in a widdershins direction and visualising the protective energy field dissipating. However, because this is a dark moon rite in which you have already cast your circle in a widdershins direction, you may prefer to call it back by walking in the opposite direction (known as 'deosil'[17]).

Allow the candle to burn out completely in a safe place such as a sink or tiled area.

It is also not uncommon for people to feel drained around this time of the lunar cycle. This is because if you have been consciously working with aligning yourself to the ebbing and flowing of the moon's energy, you will also need to allow yourself a time to rest, to turn inward, to allow yourself to replenish your own energies–just as Lady Lunar does as she withdraws herself from the skies.

Throughout time, the moon has been associated with our power within, and men, as well as women, are capable of connection with this power. The dark phase, which is associated with the Crone phase, appears in the sky during the last three days of every lunar cycle; it is a time for life-enriching endings and a prelude to new beginnings. When the dark moon appears to us, we find it much easier to shed that unnecessary emotional baggage that we carry within us and to free ourselves of those people and ideas that no longer add value to our life. This is the time when we need to cleanse ourselves of the old and unnecessary to create space so that the new can enter.

Embracing Our Own Darkness

When we look to the night's sky and see nothing, this provides us with the opportunity to go within, into our own darkness of the self, and to observe or even begin to know those parts that we cannot see clearly. The darkness of the self can be extremely confronting for people because this is often where we find the areas we have not embraced, explored or accepted in ourselves. These are aspects of our self that we may wish to hide from, yet there can be strength and beauty waiting for us to properly acknowledge or embrace.

These days, there is an increasing interest in 'shadow work', a Jungian psychological term referring to these aspects of the self that we tend to ignore, reject and hide away in our subconscious. There are many ways that you can explore your shadow side; my preference is through the use of mythology, which led me to write *Encountering the Dark Goddess: A Journey into the Shadow Realms*. Other people find that working more closely with the ebbing and flowing energies of the lunar tides can assist. The choice is completely up to the individual; it depends greatly on how deeply you wish to explore your shadow side. I always recommend, however, a degree of caution just in case hidden traumatic events arise. If they do, please see a professional, such as a counsellor or even a psychologist. If this is not an option, then even a close friend could be of benefit.

We have long been taught to fear the darkness, to fear what

may not be seen and readily available to us. Yet there is an element of awe and anticipation about the dark moon. It can be a time of great stirring deep within the core of our being because we can get in touch with the ancestors, the Old Ones, the ancient gods and goddesses. As we sit and go deep within ourselves, we can tap into the ancient wisdom that we carry today within our DNA, in our bodies. We are able to sink down deeply into the very roots not only of our being but into the ground, the earth behind us. As we continue to breathe and connect deeper and deeper, we can move down through the ancient roots and foundations and back to the ancient primordial mother, the originating goddess who birthed us all.

The dark moon can be extremely potent because it is the phase when we can connect with our deepest truth and Lady Lunar provides us with the opportunity to peel back the layers to expose what is beneath, and to investigate the progress of our soul if we so desire. The time of the dark moon is the time when the stars shine their brightest – and so too can we.

Prayer to the Dark Moon

Hail Lady Lunar, of the darkened sky
From us below do you hide
Release from me my inner fears
Free my soul from wounds and tears
Lady Lunar, reveal to me
Your inner blessings, so mote it be.

Magical Dark Moon Workings
During this phase of the moon, it is often the time to relax and turn your attention inward before the lunar cycle repeats.

Part II
Lunar Phenomenon

Lunar Phenomenon

Astrological Keys and Terms

Art thou pale for weariness
Of climbing heaven and gazing on the earth,
Wandering companionless
Among the stars that have a different birth, -
And ever changing, like a joyless eye
That finds no object work its constancy?
('To the Moon' by Percy Bysshe Shelley)[18]

If you have been using the previous section to deepen your connection with the moon, then considering what astrological sign the moon is in can add another level to your understanding and connection with Lady Lunar. I have discussed this briefly in the full moon section; however, let us dive a bit deeper into these astrological keys.

The moon leaves one sign, or house, of the zodiac and enters the next every 2 to 2.5 days. In each sign, the moon exerts unique influences on the processes of the unconscious mind, thereby affecting certain undertakings. The influences wax and wane as the moon enters each sign and takes its leave; these are further tempered by the moon phases of the signs on either side.

When the moon is in transit, that is, at the end of an astrological sign or just entering an astrological sign, it is 'void of course'. Such a period is particularly fraught with uncertainties. I discuss more about 'void of course' later in this section.

The distance the moon traverses on any given day is called a 'mansion of the moon', of which there are 24. These should not be confused with the 12 houses of the zodiac. The first mansion begins at 0° Aries, the second at about 12° or 13° Aries and so on. Each mansion also has its own influences; however, because there is not the space in this book to explain this in greater depth, if this is something you are interested in, I would recommend reading more astrologically focused books and websites, or even undertaking a course in astrology.

Every day of the month also has favourable or unfavourable aspects for particular activities. To discover auspices, you will need an ephemeris to determine the moon's location at a given day and hour. When the moon resides within the various signs, that sign influences the magical aspect of the moon, and therefore, can also have an effect on our lives. Likewise, when it comes to new or full moon rites, or other magical workings, the astrological phase of the moon can have an impact. One way of noting how the different astrological signs affect you is to complete a moon chart; information on how to do this can be found in Part III. The following list breaks down the various astrological keys and explains how they influence the moon, together with appropriate correspondences that can be used if you want to undertake specific spells and rituals that focus on these astrological keys.

Moon in Aries ♈

As the first sign of the zodiac, Aries is the pioneer. Now is the appropriate time to undertake things that deal with leadership, new beginnings, physical strength and courage. If you are fighting any battles, now is the appropriate time to make your move. Bear in mind, however, that while things may move quickly, the energy of this moon is often short-lived owing to a lack of staying power. Therefore, use this energy for short-term goals that need quick action and high energy instead of anything longer term. There is often a feeling of impatience and tempers can run hot. However, it is a good time to draw on your inner courage or even to put your foot down, reinforcing your opinion or point of view.

Aries Moon Correspondences:

- **Key words**: Leadership, authority, rebirth, willpower, independence, risk taking, aggression, restlessness
- **Focus**: Strength, vitality, energy
- **Health**: Head, face, brain
- **Ruling planet**: Mars
- **Element**: Fire
- **Incense**: Dragon's Blood
- **Botanicals**: Fennel, cumin, wormwood
- **Colours**: Burgundy, scarlet, red, crimson, orange

Moon in Taurus ♉

Taurus is closely associated with Earth, grounding, stability and patience. As this moon solidifies and manifests, it is well suited for anything connected with the physical and material world. Things begun under a Taurus moon develop slowly and build gradually. Therefore, use this energy for well-planned, long-term goals, as well as anything that you want to last. Keep in mind, however, that enterprises begun now will often be difficult to change later on. This moon also heightens an interest in creature comforts and could lead to a tendency to overindulge. It is a poor time to make changes, especially financial, and can lead to becoming stubborn if put under pressure.

Taurus Moon Correspondences:

- **Key words**: Love, security, real estate, material acquisition, money
- **Focus**: Grounding, patience, stability
- **Health**: Neck, throat, ears
- **Ruling planet**: Venus
- **Element**: Earth
- **Incense**: Rose

- **Botanicals**: Cardamom, oak moss, lotus
- **Colours**: Jade, emerald green, pink, turquoise, sapphire

Moon in Gemini ♊

The ficklest sign of the zodiac, Gemini can seem to be all over the place owing to its highly changeable nature. It is the time for exploration, when you are intrigued by the ideas and endless details, as well as multi-tasking and focusing on more communication-orientated activities. This seemingly scattered energy of the Gemini moon focuses on a constant state of evolution as curiosity fills the air, and is a good time for exchanging ideas instead of focusing on one project, or when the unfamiliar becomes fascinating. While it is a good time for meetings and being with family, there is a tendency to be flippant, indecisive and even uncertain if put under pressure.

Gemini Moon Correspondences:

- **Key words**: Communications, change of residence, writing, local travel, siblings
- **Focus**: Learning, study, evolution
- **Health**: Arms, hands, shoulders lungs
- **Ruling planet**: Mercury
- **Element**: Air
- **Incense**: Citron
- **Botanicals**: Dill, lavender, parsley
- **Colours**: Yellow, mauve, green

Moon in Cancer ♋: The moon is in its own house when it moves into the sign of Cancer, encouraging us to focus on domestic matters, the home and the heart, as well as the heart and soul of our being. Projects commenced under a Cancer moon tend to have a gentle fluid quality about them. It is the time to nurture ourselves with loving care and focus on things that really matter as opposed to making a dramatic change. Being the most fertile sign of the zodiac, use this energy for experiencing, releasing and embracing emotions that may have been buried beneath the surface, whether you engage a therapist, the ear of a good friend or take a trip out into nature. The Cancer moon can make us overindulge more easily with food and alcohol, as well as tend to be less adaptable when we find that we are under pressure.

Cancer Moon Correspondences:

- **Key words**: Home, family, domestic concerns, emotions
- **Focus**: Home, family, heart
- **Health**: Stomach, chest
- **Ruling planet**: Moon
- **Element**: Water
- **Incense**: Gardenia
- **Botanicals**: Moonwort, clary sage, lemon balm
- **Colours**: White, silver, amber

Moon in Leo ♌

When the moon enters the proud, fiery sign of Leo, a boost of power, creativity and celebration can be felt. Now is the time to focus on what will make an impact, flourish and thrive. Things begun under a Leo moon tend to take centre stage for they are bold and brash, and will stand a better chance at success. There is also a light-hearted feel to the Leo moon energy – things seem somewhat dull if they do not have a dramatic flair. So do not take things too seriously because they could turn dark, especially when the wounded pride becomes fiercely guarded. There is also a possibility of becoming arrogant and vain if put under pressure.

Leo Moon Correspondences:

- **Key words**: Authority, power over others, confidence and ego, courage, fertility, children
- **Focus**: Creativity, confidence, self-expression
- **Health**: Heart, spine, upper back
- **Ruling planet**: Sun
- **Element**: Fire
- **Incense**: Sandalwood
- **Botanicals**: Cinnamon, juniper, mistletoe
- **Colours**: Gold, orange, yellow

Moon in Virgo ♍

Virgo is the sign of efficiency and practicality. Now is the time to set things straight, to focus on matters of wellness, organisation and attending to detail. Projects begun under a Virgo moon tend to need more detail, more research and more perfecting because every glitch possible tends to come to light. Moods may become heavy and personal morals may slide as Virgo is the fault finder, focusing on areas that need improvement. However, obsessive attention to detail may be displayed as well as a greater lack of tolerance if under pressure.

Virgo Moon Correspondences:

- **Key words**: Work, service to others, intellectual matters, health, routine, dietary issues
- **Focus**: Improvement, simplification, purification
- **Health**: Nervous system, intestines
- **Ruling planet**: Mercury
- **Element**: Earth
- **Incense**: Patchouli
- **Botanicals**: Rosemary, vervain
- **Colours**: Dark grey, dark orange, dark blue

Moon in Libra ♎

With its sign being the scales of justice, the Libra moon is about balance and attempting to observe things from other side. Things commenced during this moon tend to be more changeable than at other times. Ensure that you make time for yourself and avoid conflicts whenever possible. This is a perfect time to commence projects that intend to be peaceful, in the pursuit of justice, or focus on aesthetics. Be mindful, however, if achieving a desire starts to become dishonourable, indecisive or dissatisfied.

Libra Moon Correspondences:

- **Key words:** Justice, legal issues, artistic work, partnerships, close personal relationships, decision making
- **Focus:** Balance, beauty, justice
- **Health:** Kidneys, spine, lower back
- **Ruling planet:** Venus
- **Element:** Air
- **Incense:** Rose
- **Botanicals:** Thyme, catnip, mugwort
- **Colours:** Emerald green, deep blue, magenta

Moon in Scorpio ♏

Scorpio is the most intensive sign of the zodiac. It is the time of power, whether it be building power, using it or being confronted by another person's power. This makes any project begun under a Scorpio moon take on a level of depth, intensity and power of its own, making things somewhat difficult if you change your mind at a later stage. Emotions are stirred and the energies of this moon will intensify emotional problems, such as depression or obsession. This heightened sensitivity can lead to anger, malice and even suspicion, especially with respect to financial matters. Watch for potentially destructive behaviours that could end valuable connections and even relationships.

Scorpio Moon Correspondences:

- **Key words**: Sexual matters, psychic development, secrets, transformations, revenge
- **Focus**: Power, depth, intensity
- **Health**: Bodily elimination systems, reproductive organs
- **Ruling planet**: Mars, Pluto
- **Element**: Water
- **Incense**: Frankincense
- **Botanicals**: Valerian, ginger, basil
- **Colours**: Black, crimson, red

Moon in Sagittarius ♐

Sagittarius opens doors and minds to new experiences and exotic locations. It is the time to experiment and gain experience through trying something different. Any projects commenced during a Sagittarius moon will take off, bursting with action and likely continue to expand. It is also an opportune time to focus on projects of a more financial nature as well as those that will enrich your life. This is an adventurous spirit aligned with this moon's energy that can encourage intellectual and philosophical debate. However, you will need to be mindful not to purposefully touch a nerve or show blatant disregard with respect to the beliefs of another person.

Sagittarius Moon Correspondences:

- **Key words**: Higher education, publishing, legal matters, truth, expansion, religion, spiritual matters and travel
- **Focus**: Expansion, belief, experience
- **Health**: Liver, hips, thighs
- **Ruling planet**: Jupiter
- **Element**: Fire

- **Incense**: Carnation
- **Botanicals**: Clove, sage, pennyroyal
- **Colours**: Purple, red, royal blue

Moon in Capricorn ♑

The Capricorn moon is the business moon as the sea goat sets its mind to climb from the ocean to the highest mountain. Now is the time for focusing and certainty. Projects commenced under this moon will progress exactly as planned and will reach the intended goal. However, such progress should not be rushed, especially when obstacles are encountered. Perseverance is the key, together with patience. Anything unplanned will likely go nowhere. The energy of the Capricorn is heavy, practical and more logical and is lacking empathy and emotions. There may be a tendency for depression, pessimism and frustration owing to the limitations and restrictions that can be felt. However, it is a good time for discipline and hard work.

Capricorn Moon Correspondences:

- **Key words**: Career, aims, goals, achievement, politics, organisations
- **Focus**: Determination, structure, plan
- **Health**: Bones, joints, knees, skin, teeth
- **Ruling planet**: Saturn
- **Element**: Earth
- **Incense**: Musk
- **Botanicals**: Vervain, comfrey, nightshade
- **Colours**: Red, brown, dark green

Moon in Aquarius ♒

Aquarius is the sign of the rebel and the free thinker. When the moon moves into this sign, things are set to change. Anything commenced during this moon is highly unlikely to turn out according to plan; however, it is a perfect time to break free from restrictions and the influences of other people and try something new. The Aquarius moon is a great time for forming new friendships and networking connections, as well as planning for the future. However, an excessive emphasis on ideas can lead to disappointment if they are too unreachable.

Aquarius Moon Correspondences:

- **Key words**: Scientific issues, freedom, originality, mental clarity, problem solving, inventing, overcoming bad habits, friendships, socialising
- **Focus**: Change, freedom, connection
- **Health**: Circulation, ankles, calves
- **Ruling planet**: Uranus, Saturn
- **Element**: Air
- **Incense**: Frankincense
- **Botanicals**: Lavender, mace, mint
- **Colours**: Azure blue, cobalt blue, light blue

Moon in Pisces ♓

The last sign of the zodiac is Pisces the fish, which has the reputation of being the most spiritual sign because it is more connected with the unseen realms. While projects that are commenced under the Pisces moon tend to grow and spread quickly, they can lack focus and definition, even if goals are set, and could even evolve into something completely different. The energies of this moon encourage us towards nostalgia, empathy and imagination. This is a contemplative and wandering feeling that could lead to confusion, opening us up to daydreaming, forgetfulness and even the possibility of being manipulated by other people if we allow the lunar tides to pull us too far away from reality.

Pisces Moon Correspondences:

- **Key words**: Dreams, telepathy, creative arts, addiction, disillusionment
- **Focus**: Openness, vision, imagination
- **Health**: Lymphatic system, feet
- **Ruling planet**: Neptune, Jupiter
- **Element**: Water
- **Incense**: Carnation
- **Botanicals**: Anise, eucalyptus, water lily
- **Colours**: Lavender, sea green, pearl

One website that I use to ascertain what astrological sign the moon is in is Astro-Seek.com. This site allows you to search the monthly moon phases and lists eclipses and other information based on wherever you live in the world. Other sites can be found in the resource section at the end of this book.

Natal Moon Signs

When looking at what sign the moon is in, it can also be beneficial to observe how this compares with our own personal natal moon sign – that is, what astrological sign the moon was in at the time of our birth. Natal moon signs can reveal much about our own inner self and provide insight into the way we handle our emotions and fears and how we feel about things. This is because during such times, our actions are more than likely to be influenced by emotion and instinct as opposed to reality.

Natal moon signs are governed by their astrological make-up in the cosmos and are connected with one of the four elements: earth, air, fire and water. To discover your personal natal moon sign, you can use internet sites such as Astrodienst, which provide free charts. All you need is the date, time and location of your birth. If you do not know the exact time, you could put midday or midnight to provide a general chart.

Once you have your natal chart, take note of any significant astrological aspects. Then, take note of when the moon moves into the same sign. The location of Lady Lunar affects us by pulling on our emotions just as she pulls on the tides of the ocean.

Another influence that the moon can have on us at the time of our birth is the phase that it is in. Web sites like Astro Style (https://astrostyle.com/cosmic-calculators/moon-phase) can help in finding out what your natal moon phase is, even if you are not sure of that exact time. Be mindful that as the moon changes signs every 2 to 2 ½ days, if you do not know the exact time this may not be 100% accurate. Therefore, you might need to play around with the times. While Astro Style offer a more in-depth description of moon phases, a brief summary follows:

- **New Moon**: With the sun and moon being perfectly aligned, your heart and mind are also in harmony. You like trying new things, visiting new places and appear to be overflowing with enthusiasm, vitality and exciting new ideas. There is a childlike innocence, wonder and curiosity that you never seem to lose as you get older. The downside to this strong creative ability is that you get distracted easily and tend to move from one project to the next without finishing anything. You are also not able to see things from a different perspective, and even when offering advice, this will come from your own experience therefore not always allowing alternative viewpoints.
- **Waxing Crescent Moon**: While you are also adventurous and full of curiosity, there is a degree of conservatism when it comes to taking risk or even trying new things. Personal security is important so you may prefer to stay in your comfort zone which can hinder your independence. As such, it is important that you accept failure and even pain as potential side-effects and allow yourself to take more risks that will enhance your life.

- **First Quarter Moon:** You tend to be a bit of a protagonist, enjoy challenges to the extent that the more they are, the more excited you become. You tend to identify and resolve problems before they get too large. The downside is that you may have some difficulty dealing with any issues that require patience.
- **Waxing Gibbous Moon:** You are very caring, nurturing, and calming especially with those close to you, who you tend to guide and inspire. This can lead to a degree of perfectionism when it comes to how you see yourself. Remember that no one will ever truly be perfect and it is in this imperfection that person growth can be achieved.
- **Full Moon:** If you were born under a full moon that your life may be influenced by internal struggles between which is logical (the sun) and your heart's desire (the moon). This may result in you being rather inconsistent or indecisive to those who do not know you. Your friends, however, know to expect the unexpected. Success can be gained when you attune to the rhythms both internally as well as those around you. Listen to your intuition and be honest with yourself.
- **Waning Gibbous Moon:** You may seem wiser than your years with an innate desire to understand and explain things, making you a great teacher. The challenge is that you can come off as arrogant and condescending when trying to get your message across. Keep in mind that people may already have a deeper or different understanding of the topic. Your core challenge is to overcome self-actualization.
- **Last Quarter Moon:** While you have no fear of the present or the future, you do tend to have a strong attachment to the past and as such, this may prevent you from moving forward with ease. While reminiscing can bring you happiness, and generally you are immensely loyal and

kind, your relationship with the past may be perceived as absentmindedness or even rudeness. There is also the tendency to hang on to grudges and unpleasant events which can affect your mental health. Remember that the present is equally deserving of your attention.

- **Waning Crescent Moon**: You tend to be very in touch with your intuitive side, recalling dreams and visions as well as having a rather active imagination. Your insights are often deep, making you appear somewhat mystical that compliment your rather unconventional hobbies, behaviour and opinions. This may make you somewhat of a loner as many people may find you too eccentric to relate. Embrace your uniqueness and share it with likeminded people who will appreciate you for who you are.

Cosmic Relationships

In addition to discovering what astrological sign the moon is in, you might also like to pay attention to the relationship to other cosmic bodies, such as planets and even asteroids, because these can also affect your ritual and magical workings. Depending on what astrological source you use to access your lunar information, you may come across mention of the following terms:

- **Conjunction**: Celestial objects are in the same degree and same sign and aligned from our point on Earth.
- **Opposition**: 180° angle to each other, can intensify interplanetary dynamics.
- **Sextile**: 60° angle to each other, peaceful, harmonious influence.
- **Square**: 90° angle to each other, challenging aspect but for some people, when the going gets tough, they get going and this can lead to a breakthrough.
- **Trine**: 120° angle and semi-sextile 30° angle to each other – both of these are harmonious influences.

- **Quincunx**: 150° angle to each other can present a hurdle to overcome.

Whether you apply this knowledge in your own ritual and spellcasting is entirely up to you. For example, just because the moon is waxing, the time associated with bringing things into your life, of putting your wishes and desires out into the universe, and so on, it does not necessarily mean that you should actually do this, especially if we look beneath the surface, or in this case, to the heavens above. Other planets could be in retrograde, in opposition, or even squared and that will have an effect on how our lunar magic may materialise. Some cosmic events may actually imply that a waxing moon may not be the most auspicious time to ask for something, especially if any releasing or renewal work has not yet been undertaken.

Before I design a lunar ritual, I tend to visit a number of astrological sites to see whether there are any other cosmic influences that I should be aware of. Some of these sites even provide monthly forecasts that can be used when planning future rituals.

Void of Course of the Moon

As mentioned previously, when the moon departs from one sign of the zodiac and enters the next, it is referred to as the 'void of course' and the transition can be a tricky time. The moon exerts a certain influence while it occupies a sign; however, when in transit, it has nothing to affect. Therefore, the moon's influence on Earth can feel somewhat chaotic. Odd things may happen, behaviours may seem erratic, objects may be misplaced and mistakes may be made, and we may even lose our way.

Decisions made when the moon is void can easily go sour. Newly purchased objects may break, may become defective or even left unused. Agreements that seem rock solid change later. Those who are accident prone are likely to have a mishap. Travel is subject to delays, cancellations and accidents. Therefore, exercise caution during these times. If possible, stick to routine matters and projects already underway. Avoid launching new projects, signing contracts, making major decisions (especially financial ones) and travelling.

The moon goes void approximately every 2 to 2.5 days. Some void periods last only for a few minutes, but most last several hours, with some lasting for a day or even longer.

When a Planet Is in Retrograde

Retrograde is an astronomical term used to describe the movement of a planet when from Earth it appears to be moving backwards; this, however, is an illusion because in reality, all planets revolve around the sun in the same direction. The appearance of this retrograde movement occurs because of the different speeds at which each planet is travelling.

One planet, in particular, that tends to greatly affect us when it appears retrograde in our skies is Mercury, the planet that rules communication, travel and technology. It is not uncommon for emails to go astray during this time or to experience miscommunication. Care is often recommended when signing contracts while Mercury is in retrograde, or at least reading contracts, or any other important documents, very carefully before signing.

The moon, however, never appears in retrograde.

Super Moons

A super moon is the coincidence of the full moon appearing larger than normal because it has reached its full phase on the part of its elliptical orbit that brings it closest to Earth. The technical term for this occurrence is the 'perigee syzygy' of the Earth–moon–sun relationship. During the super moon, the full moon is less than 360,000 km away from Earth.

The term 'super moon' is a fairly modern term that is believed to have been coined only some 30 years ago by US astrologer

Richard Nolle and is not a term found within astronomy. The association of the moon with both oceanic and crustal tides has led to the belief that during super moons, there is a heightened risk of earthquakes, volcanic eruptions and even larger than normal tides occurring. Little actual evidence supports this theory.

The opposite phenomenon to a super moon is known as an 'apogee syzygy', a micro moon, which is a term that is not commonly used. During a micro moon, the moon appears to be some 14% smaller because it is at its furthest distance from Earth, some 400,000 km, on its elliptical orbit. Therefore, it appears to be less bright.

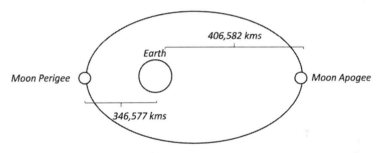

Figure 2: Super Moons

In reality, however, there is no difference in the actual size of the moon regardless of whether it is a super moon, a micro moon or an ordinary full moon.

> *Soon as the evening shades prevail,*
> *The moon takes up the wondrous tale,*
> *And nightly to the listening earth*
> *Repeats the story of her birth;*
> *While all the stars that round her burn,*
> *And all the planets in their turn,*
> *Confirm the tidings as they roll,*
> *And spread the truth from pole to pole.*[19]

Blue Moons, Black Moons and Dark Moon Lilith

There are a number of interpretations as to what a 'blue moon' refers to; the first two are in connection with timing. A 'seasonal blue moon' is the name used to refer to 'the third full moon in an [astronomical] season that has four full moons, thus correcting the timing of the last month of the season that would have otherwise been expected too early'.[20] A 'seasonal blue moon' takes place every two or three years.

More commonly, however, it refers to the second full moon in the same calendar month. This happens because the lunar cycle is 29.5 days; the phases of the moon gradually slip backwards through the progression of the Gregorian calendar until a full moon appears near the beginning of the month and again at the end of the month. This type of blue moon is also referred to as a 'monthly blue moon' and is more likely in months that have 31 days (i.e. January, March, May, July, August, October and December).

It is interesting to note that the first recorded use of the term 'blue moon' dates from 1528, when it originally meant 'betrayer moon', which is completely the opposite to its esoteric and magical connection today. Further, it has only been since 1940 that the term 'blue moon' has been used for the second full moon in a month that has two full moons.

There are also times when the moon appears to be blue in colour. Such blue moons occur when dust particles and pollution in Earth's atmosphere filter more light at the red end of the colour spectrum than at the blue end. The longer wavelengths, including red and yellow, scatter, while the shorter wavelengths, including blue and green, intensify. This gives the moon a blue or green appearance against the night sky, especially if it is low on the horizon, where its light is subject to the greatest refraction by the atmosphere. The moon 'turned' blue following the volcanic eruption of Krakatoa, Indonesia, in 1883.

When there are two dark moons in one calendar month, the

second dark moon is sometimes referred to as a 'black moon'. This occurs when February misses a full moon, which is due to the lunar synodic period (the length of time it takes the moon to return to a phase) taking 29.5 days. The flow-on effect from February having no dark moon is that there will be two dark moons in a later month.

For some people who follow a more Earth-centric spiritual belief system, the time of a black moon is considered extremely powerful and a most effective time when it comes to crafting magic. This is because of the rarity of such a moon. The black moon is also considered an opportunity for inner truth and to undertake some deep soul work in order to see your inner self clearly. It is the time to listen to the voice you have tried to ignore during times when you were too busy to pay attention.

Within astronomy, the term 'Black Moon Lilith' (or 'Dark Moon Lilith') refers to a mathematical point in space that does not actually exist as a physical point in space; instead, it is a point that describes the distance between Earth and the moon. When drawn, the astrological glyph used is a right-facing black crescent underpinned by a cross.

As mentioned previously, when the moon is furthest away from Earth, this is the 'lunar apogee', which places the Black Moon Lilith in conjunction with the moon. Opposite to this is the 'lunar perigee', when the moon is closest to Earth. During this time, the Black Moon Lilith is opposite to the moon.

In mythology, Lilith, the first wife of the biblical Adam, has been depicted as a succubus, a night demon and even a baby killer. She is also a dark goddess who entices us to break free from society niceties or taboos that surround sex, death, addiction, transformation and the occult. Night terrors and UFO abductions are also connected with Lilith.[21] Being described by some astrologers as a 'ghost' or 'shadow' moon, the Black Moon Lilith tends to be more connected with sex – not sex through courting and procreation, but the sexual power plays, politics and even psychology of sex when used as a weapon.[22] Other astrologers connect the Black Moon Lilith with raw feminine energy that reminds us to stand up for ourselves, to speak our true voice and to withstand situations that may be somewhat uncomfortable, yet necessary, with respect to our spiritual journey.

The Black Moon Lilith is further observed as representing the void and the darkness that descends prior to any change or transformation. While this darkness may feel intimidating at first, the energy emerging from it will give us the confidence to stand in our own power and remember that light will always return. At times, we simply need to go through the dark void for the necessary transformation to occur, much like a caterpillar needing to retreat into the darkness of its cocoon to undergo its destined transformation and rebirth into a butterfly.

Many astrologers indicate that it takes just under nine years for the Black Moon Lilith to complete one full resolution through all 12 signs of the zodiac.

Lunar and Solar Eclipses

To the ancient people, the two most important celestial objects, the sun and the moon, fostered and regulated all life on Earth. If anything occurred to threaten the existence or function of these two bodies, chaos and catastrophe would surely follow. Whenever the sun and moon seemed to disappear from the sky or become covered with blood (for that is what seems to happen during an eclipse), it was feared that the world would end. Therefore, the word 'eclipse' (from the Greek *ekleipsis*) implies fear and means 'failure' in the sense of something going wrong. This may have very well stemmed from our prehistoric ancestors' reactions to when the sun or moon disappeared from sight.

There are two kinds of eclipses, lunar and solar, and the moon plays a key role in both. Solar eclipses always occur at the new moon when the sun and moon are in the exact same part of the sky. At the new moon, the moon is invisible because it is close to the sun. Solar eclipses tend to be a more awesome spectacle because the sun seems to disappear from the sky owing to the moon coming between Earth and the sun, resulting in the blunt point of the darkest part of the shadow (umbra) moving over the rotating Earth. Sometimes the sun vanishes completely from view, while at other times just a bright ring (the penumbra) flashes in the sky, causing a partial solar eclipse. There are four types of solar eclipses – total, annual, partial and hybrid – which I will discuss later.

Lunar eclipses tend to be less frequent and occur at the full moon, when Earth intervenes between the moon and the sun, enabling the moon to enter Earth's shadow. The moon changes colour, usually becoming coppery, sometimes deepening to red or rust. It can stay that way for as long as 90 minutes, whereas the entire lunar eclipse can last up to four hours, sometimes even longer, as Earth and moon slowly move in relation to each other.

Both types of eclipses are simple matters; their mystery and magic is in the eye of the beholder.

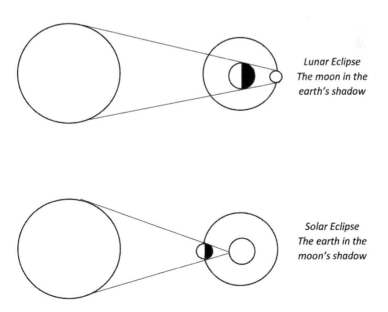

Lunar Eclipse
The moon in the
earth's shadow

Solar Eclipse
The earth in the
moon's shadow

Figure 3: Lunar and Solar Eclipses

Eclipses occur because the orbit of the moon is tilted around 5° from the ecliptic (orbital planet) of Earth's orbit around the sun. The moon travels either slightly above or slightly below that of Earth. Where the two orbital planes intersect, these two points are referred to as 'lunar nodes'. Depending on the direction that the moon is heading in, they are either 'ascending' (from south to north) or 'descending' (from north to south) and are often referred to as the 'tail of the dragon' when the head is ascending and the tail is descending. I will discuss nodes in more detail in a moment. For the time being, let us just focus on the eclipses.

Just as the moon passes through the two nodes once a month, the sun passes through each lunar node once every year. This is why each type of eclipse usually takes place twice a year, approximately six months apart. In some cases, however, a year will not have a second lunar eclipse. The lunar eclipse can always be observed from all locations on the night side of Earth (when the full moon is above the horizon), while a solar eclipse can only be seen on the day side of Earth in a narrow zone (where the shadow of the moon falls). This narrow zone is approximately 250 km wide.

When lunar eclipses occur, they can be seen from all points of Earth where the moon is visible. In a lunar eclipse, the full moon passes through the shadow of Earth at another node, cutting itself off from the sun's rays. The moon darkens in colour and, in some cases, may seem to disappear.

The four different types of a lunar eclipse are:

- **Total lunar eclipse**: This is when Earth's full (umbra) shadow falls on the moon. The moon will not completely disappear from sight; however, there is an eerie darkness that makes it easy to miss if you were not looking for the eclipse. The moon often appears red in colour due to the light refraction of Earth's atmosphere.
- **Partial lunar eclipse**: This is when the sun, Earth and

moon are not quite perfectly aligned, and Earth's shadow appears to take a bite out of the moon by causing a significant shadow.

- **Penumbral lunar eclipse:** This is the least interesting type of eclipse because the moon is in Earth's faint outer shadow (penumbral) causing only a partial darkening of a portion of the moon. This type of an eclipse often goes unnoticed except by seasoned sky watchers.

- **Total penumbral lunar eclipse:** This is when the moon is completely shadowed by the penumbra, however, the umbra (the darkest and central part of the shadow that the earth casts on the moon) is not touched.

There is also a selenelion, or horizontal, eclipse which only happens when both the sun and the moon are visible during the eclipse.

The Danjon Scale, created by French astronomer Andre Louis Danjon, measures the brightness of a lunar eclipse by indicating the amount of sunlight that is refracted through Earth's atmosphere before it indirectly illuminates the moon and is returned to Earth.

0   It is a very dark eclipse where the moon is almost invisible.

1   Dark eclipse with a grey or brownish discolouration which can be distinguishable but with a degree of difficulty.

2   Deep red or rust coloured eclipse that has a very dark central shadow; however, the outer edges of the umbra are bright.

3   Brick red eclipse where the umbral shadow usually has a bright, almost yellow rim.

4   Very bright, copper-red or even orange eclipse where the umbral shadow has a bluish, very bright rim.

Closer to my part of the world, on Badu (Mulgrave Island in the Torres Strait between Australia and Papua New Guinea), a lunar eclipse is known as *Merlpal Maru Pathanu*, meaning 'the ghost has taken the spirit of the moon'. It was also viewed as an omen for war; on the northernmost Torres Strait Island, Boigu, men were reported to wear special headdresses and perform special ceremonies to ascertain which direction an attack was coming from.[23] Within the Dreaming of the Arrernte People of the central region of Australia's Northern Territory, a total lunar eclipse is caused by the 'Moon Man' hiding his face behind some possum fur.

A solar eclipse occurs when the new moon lines up directly between the sun and Earth at one node, cutting off the sun's rays. The moon appears black as it passes in front of the sun. Even though the moon is much smaller than the sun, it appears to be nearly the same size in the sky because it is so much closer to Earth. The sun returns to full luminosity as the moon passes away.

Total solar eclipses are so spectacular that some people will travel thousands of miles just for a few minutes of one of nature's greatest shows. This is because they can only be seen from certain portions of Earth that are in the proper line of sight for the blocking effect to occur. Such was the case in the late 18th century when Mabel Loomis Todd (the wife of US astronomer David Peck Todd) described what she experienced in rather poetic detail: as the 'dark body of the moon gradually steals its silent way across the brilliant sun ... a sense of uneasiness seems gradually to steal over all life ... bird songs diminish, grasshoppers fall quiet and a suggestion of chill crosses the air. Darker and darker grows the landscape'.[24]

As the eclipse takes hold, Todd describes that 'the world might well be dead and cold and turned to ashes ... a lull suddenly awakens into a strange wind, blowing with unnatural effect. Then out of the darkness, gruesome but sublime, flashes of the glory of the incomparable corona, a silvery, soft, unearthly light, with radiant streamers, stretching at times millions of uncomprehended miles into space, while the rosy, flame-like prominences skirt the black rim of the moon in ethereal splendor'.[25]

The earliest record of a solar eclipse can be found in the ancient Chinese *Shujing* (or *Book of Documents*) in which two court astronomers, Hsi and Ho, had become drunk, unaware that a solar eclipse was about to occur. In the aftermath, Zhong Kang, the fourth emperor of the Xia dynasty ordered that the astronomers have their heads chopped off as a form of punishment. The eclipse in question took place on 22 October in 2,134 BCE.

The biblical reference 'I will cause the sun to go down at noon, and I will darken the earth in the clear day' (Amos 8:9) is believed by biblical scholars to relate to an eclipse observed in the ancient Assyrian city of Nineveh on 15 June 763 BCE. While an Assyria tablet attests to the event, this does not necessarily point to the legitimacy of this claim.

In the early 6th century BCE, during the five-year war between the Lydians and the Medes in what is now modern-day Turkey, the Greek sage Thales of Miletus foretold that a time would come when day would turn to night. As predicted, on 17 May 603 BCE, an eclipse occurred, causing the sun to fade away. Believing this to be a sign from the gods, a truce was called. As mentioned previously in this book, Thales was knowledgeable, at least to a certain degree, of the cosmic happenings.

A solar eclipse tends to relate to a fated new beginning – something that happens to us – and can present itself in the form of an opportunity or a demand to adjust to a new situation. Sometimes an annular eclipse occurs when the moon is a bit further away from Earth than usual. This means that it does not fully cover the sun, resulting in a ring of fire or halo effect. In metaphysical thought, this fertile union of the sun and moon is considered a window to the divine. This could explain why many images of saints or other important spiritual or religious figures are depicted with a halo around their heads, as a way of drawing attention to the message that they have.

As mentioned previously, a solar eclipse occurs when the moon moves between Earth and the sun, whereby the moon casts a shadow over Earth. A solar eclipse can only take place during a new moon; whether the alignment produces a total solar eclipse, a partial solar eclipse or an annular solar eclipse depends on several factors, all explained below.

Some astronomers consider that the fact an eclipse occurs at all is rather a fluke of celestial mechanics and time. This is because ever since the moon was formed about 4.5 billion years ago, it has been slowly moving away from Earth at a rate of about 4 cm (1.6 inches) per year. At this point in time, the moon is a perfect distance to appear as if it were the exact same size as the sun in our sky, and therefore, is able to block it out. However, this may not always be the case in millenniums to come.

The why and how of the eclipses' occurrence were unknown in earlier times. This lack of understanding of cosmic events gave birth to many myths and legends that attempted to explain them. Native Americans believed the moon was hunted and caught by huge dogs. The Chinese believed a lunar eclipse was the work of hungry dragons that ate the moon. In many Asian cultures, it was also common belief that a noise made by banging gongs, pans and kettles would frighten away the dragon, demon or evil spirit that was devouring the sun or the moon.

In Romanian folklore, eclipses were said to have caused by creatures called 'varcolaci' that ate the sun and moon, whereas in Norse mythology we find the Fenrir wolf, the son of God Loki and the giantess Angrboda.

In 'The Binding of Fenrir', the Aesir Gods raised Fenrir to keep him under their control and prevent him from wreaking havoc. However, because he grew at an astonishingly fast rate, the gods decided to chain him up. After their first two attempts failed, the gods convinced Fenrir that the chains were only a game to test his strength. On the third attempt, dwarves were commissioned to forge the strongest chain ever built, which resulted in Fenrir being unable to break free of his bonds. It is said that when Ragnarok (the end of the world) occurs, Fenrir will break free and run throughout the world with his lower jaw against the ground and his upper jaw in the sky, devouring everything in his path.

Blood-Red Moon

As mentioned above, sometimes the moon may appear a red or coppery colour during a total portion of an eclipse. What makes this possible is that while the moon is in total shadow, some light from the sun can pass through Earth's atmosphere. Although other colours in the spectrum are blocked and scattered by Earth's atmosphere, the red light tends to make it through easier.

According to NASA, the exact colour that the moon appears to be depends on the amount of dust and clouds in the atmosphere. If, for example, there has been a recent volcanic eruption, then the moon will appear a darker shade of red.

Christopher Columbus was said to have leveraged a blood-red eclipse in 1504 to his advantage during his fourth and final voyage to the New World. Armed with an almanac, Columbus was aware that there would be a lunar eclipse on 29 February 1504. Seven months earlier, having already been forced to abandon two of his ships due to their being eaten by shipworms, he ended up beaching his last two ships in Jamaica on 25 June 1503. Although the local inhabitants initially looked after them, as time went on, they grew weary of providing hospitality. Some members of Columbus's crew mutinied and ended up robbing and murdering some of the Jamaicans. Columbus then met with the local chief and told him that their Christian God was angry that food was no longer being supplied, and to expect a sign of God's displeasure three nights later when the full moon would appear 'inflamed with wrath'. Indeed, in three nights' time, a blood-red moon appeared in the sky, and according to an account made by Columbus's son, the local people were terrified and provided enough provisions to keep the crew fed until help arrived the following November that enabled Columbus and his crew to return to Spain.

North and South Nodes

As mentioned previously, the nodes are the two points through which the moon travels during its elliptical journey around Earth. In astrology, our life purpose is believed to be encoded in the moon's north and south nodes. The north node is said to represent our karmic paths and show us the lessons that we come in this life time to learn, whereas the south node reveals the challenges, fears and even past traumas as well as the gifts that we bring into this life from previous lifetimes. In other words, the north node points to our fate or destiny while the south node reflects on our past lives. The north node is also referred to as the 'true node' because it shows our life's purpose as it appears in our natal chart at the time of our birth.

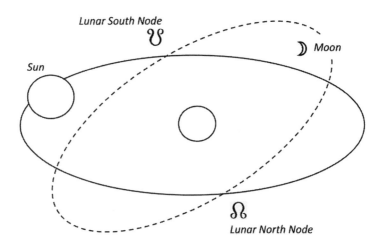

Figure 4: Lunar South and North Nodes

As these nodes appear opposite each other and are mathematical points as opposed to being actual planets, if your north node is in Capricorn, for example, then your south node will be in Cancer.

I find it interesting to note that the nodes are sometimes referred to as the 'head' or the 'tail' of the dragon by astrologers. Considering the Chinese folklore of the moon being eaten by hungry dragons as a way of explaining a lunar eclipse, I cannot help but wonder if there is some connection.

Out-of-Bounds Moon

As mentioned previously, as the sun travels around the zodiac on the ecliptic, it reaches a maximum northern declination (23°N 27') at the Tropic of Cancer (marking the summer solstice in the Northern Hemisphere and winter solstice in the Southern Hemisphere) and a maximum southern declination (23°S 27') at the tropic of Capricorn (marking the winter solstice in the Northern Hemisphere and summer solstice in the Southern Hemisphere). The declination is measured by the tilt of Earth along its axis as it orbits the sun. The planets normally travel within that band of degrees, so if a planet travels beyond the ecliptic, or beyond 23°27' to the north or south, it is considered out of bounds.

Within astrology terms, if a planet is considered 'out of bounds', it is no longer under the guidance, or rule, of the sun. This means that the planet deviates from normal expression, becoming somewhat exaggerated, unusual or even unconventional. Within an astrological chart, such energy can manifest as a remarkable talent or gift, or as inappropriate or extreme behavioural patterns.

The moon tends to have its own rhythm. For 9 or 10 years, it will stay inside the sun's ecliptic boundary (as it has done from 2011 until 2020). Then for the next 9 or 10 years, it will tend to go out of bounds several times a month. Astrologers have also found that during the peak years when the moon travels to its extreme out-of-bounds declination, this occurs when the nodes are near 0° Aries and Libra. In other words, it is possible that people born with the nodes in Aries and Libra may also have the natal moon at this extreme out of bounds.

People who have an out-of-bounds natal moon are said to be extremely intuitive and empathic in nature, and have rather transparent emotional boundaries. They may even have issues surrounding food and security.

The Lunar Standstill

Every 18.6 years, the angle between Earth's equator and the moon's orbit reaches a maximum of 28°36', which is the total of Earth's inclination (23°27') and the moon's inclination (5°09'). When this occurs, it is known as a 'major lunar standstill'. Around this time, the moon's latitude will vary from −28°36' to +28°36' and the centre of the moon's disc will only be above the horizon every day for latitudes less than 90°−28°36' or 61°24'.

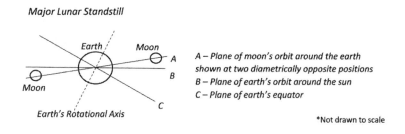

Major Lunar Standstill

A – Plane of moon's orbit around the earth shown at two diametrically opposite positions
B – Plane of earth's orbit around the sun
C – Plane of earth's equator

*Not drawn to scale

Figure 5: Major Lunar Standstill

A little over nine years later, the angle between Earth's equator and the moon's orbit will reach its minimum, that being 18°20'. When this occurs, it is known as a 'minor lunar standstill'. During this time, the centre of the moon's disc can be seen above the horizon every day as far north and as far south as 90°−18°20', or 71°40', latitude.

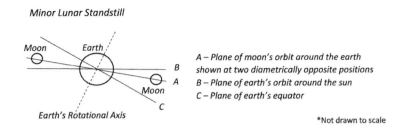

Figure 6: Minor Lunar Standstill

There are ancient sites that are specifically aligned with the lunar standstill. Stonehenge on Salisbury Plain, England, is one such site. Here, the stones and sightlines of this 5,000-year-old structure make it uniquely both a solar and a lunar calendar, as well as an observatory that indicates the summer solstice sunrise, winter solstice sunset, southernmost moonrise and northernmost moonset. At the latitude of Stonehenge, the angle between the winter solstice sunset and southernmost moonrise directions is exactly 90°.

In the Chaco Canyon, in northwestern New Mexico, a 1,000-year-old solar and lunar calendar is located on top of Fajada Butte. Discovered in 1977 and inaccessible except by ropes, at noon on the solstices and equinoxes, a dagger of light (referred to as the 'Sun Dagger') pierces a spiral petroglyph carved into the rock face of the cliff. The same spiral petroglyph has been shown to also mark the major and minor standstills of the moon. The Sun Dagger is considered the best example of a culture keeping track of the sun as well as the 18.6-year cycle of the moon.

Another site is that of Callanish, situated on the Isle of Lewis, in western Scotland. Consisting of a number of stone circles across a peat bog, Callanish (*Calanais* in Gaelic) is part of a sacred landscape where sacred ceremonies were believed to have taken place that involved bones of the dead being taken along an 80-metre-long stone avenue before their spirits were released within the biggest stone circle. The main circle of the Callanish complex is the Callanish II. This 5,000-year-old solar and lunar calendar and observatory is where the stone alignments indicate the northern moonrise and the summer solstice sunrise. The full moon nearest summer solstice appears only 3.5° above the horizon from Callanish and is viewed through the stones. During the lunar standstill, the moon appears to walk across Earth every 18.6 (nearly 19) years.

From Callanish II a series of hills that can be seen on the horizon is collectively referred to as 'Sleeping Beauty' (or *Cailleach na Mointeach* by the Gaelic-speaking locals, meaning 'The Old Woman of the Moors'). During the lunar standstill, the moon rises over Sleeping Beauty and creeps along the horizon before setting behind another hill.

If there is a cloudless night at the time, an extraordinary optical illusion occurs. If a person stands on a stone close to the circle at the point when the moon is about to set, their silhouette is back-projected onto the moon. At first the figure is tiny but then it grows until it appears bigger than the moon itself.

I was not able to travel to Callanish to witness the last lunar standstill, in 2006. I did, however, manage to visit the site in 2013, when I was fortunate to witness a sunset over Sleeping Beauty Mountain from Callanish. Maybe I will be fortunate to visit the Scottish Outer Hebridean islands for the next lunar standstill in April 2025.

Part III
Moon Magic

Thy shadow, earth, from pole to central sea,
Now steals along upon the moon's meek shine
In even monochrome and curving line
Of imperturbable serenity.

How shall I link such sun-cast symmetry
With the torn troubled form I know as thine,
That profile, placid as a brow divine,
With continents of moil and misery?

And can immense mortality but throw
So small a shade, and heaven's high human scheme
Be hemmed within the coasts yon arc implies?

Is such the stellar gauge of earthly show,
Nation at war with nation, brains that teem,
Heroes, and women fairer than the skies?
('At a Lunar Eclipse' by Thomas Hardy)[26]

Moon Magic

The Origins of the Moon

Dreamtime stories are specific stories that are passed down by Australian Aboriginal people for generations to explain natural phenomena. The following is a Dreamtime story from Cape York, northern Queensland, that shares how the moon came about.

Many years ago, people realised that a light was needed at night-time because they found it difficult to walk around or to hunt. The sun lit up their daytime – something was needed to light up the night. They held a meeting, and one idea was to collect a huge pile of firewood during the daytime hours and set fire to it just as the sun set. The fire would be big enough to light up the bush so that they could hunt and walk around and have corroborees (a specific form of ritual that is an interface between humanity and the Dreaming). Most of the people thought that this idea was impractical.

One member of the tribe had a great idea: Make a special boomerang that shines and throw it high into the sky. This boomerang would give enough light to allow people and animals to see at night. They made a giant boomerang. People tried to throw it high into the sky. They tried but they just could not throw it high enough.

A very thin, old, weak man then stepped forward and politely asked if he could try. Everyone laughed at him when they saw his weak, thin arms. One of the Elders was a kind and wise man and he said the old man should be allowed to throw the boomerang. And throw the boomerang the old man did. It went higher and higher and higher, and finally stayed up in the sky as the moon, shining down onto the people. And the shape of the boomerang can still be seen in the moon every month.

Moon Magic

If I command the moon, it will come down;
and if I wish to withhold the day, night will linger over my head; and
again,
if I wish to embark on the sea, I need no ship,
and if I wish to fly through the air, I am free from my weight.[27]

Moon magic is a personal art, even though it has basic guidelines. In ancient times, it is believed that witches held the position of the moon priests or priestesses, and in coastal regions and on islands, they were also known as sea priests or priestesses. After all, witchcraft, in particular contemporary witchcraft, is often described as being a 'lunar cult'. The use of water from the sea was an important aspect in moon magic, with salt being a crystal form. The 'charging' of water, and the release of the 'charge' through evaporation, was an important aspect.

The 'essence' of the power used in moon magic originates among the stars. The sun draws in the stellar influences and transmits them into our solar system. The planets within our system absorb this energy, which then merges with their own vibrations or energies. The planets, in turn, then emanate a composite energy within our solar system. Each planet's energy, or vibratory pattern, is unique and influences other planetary bodies and forces within each planet's sphere of influence. This is the basis of astrology and planetary correspondences in magic. The moon absorbs, condenses and channels all of these forces, which are then carried to our planet.

Heinrich Cornelius Agrippa, a 15th century magician, understood these principles:

But the moon, the nearest to the heavenly influences, by the swiftness of her course, is joined to the sun, and the other planets and stars, as a conception, bringing them forth to the inferior world, as being next to itself, for all the stars have influence on it, being the last receiver, which afterwards communicates the influence of all superiors to these inferiors, and pours them forth upon the earth.[28]

Aradia, the goddess of the Streghe (Italian witches), allegedly told her followers to seek the moon above all others, for the purposes of magic. In the closing prayer of the full moon ritual are these words:

O' Goddess of the moon ... teach us your ancient mysteries ... that the Holy Strega spoke of, for I believe the Strega's story, when she told us to entreat Thee, told us when we seek for Knowledge, to seek and find Thee above all others.[29]

Agrippa also seemed to have understood this when he wrote:

Therefore, her [the moon's] motion is to be observed before the others, as the parent of all conception ... hence it is, that without the moon intermediating, we cannot at any time attract the power of the superiors.[30]

Agrippa was referring to the moon being a focal point of all power on Earth. Without the moon, we cannot make use of the universal forces beyond her.

Doreen Valiente, a High Priestess of Gardnerian witchcraft (a style of witchcraft named after Gerald Gardner), wrote a number of devotional prayers and hymns to the moon goddess, including the following invocation:

Diana, queen of night, in all your beauty bright,
Shine on us here,
And with your silver beam, unlock the gate of dream;
Rise bright and clear.

On earth and sky and sea, your magic mystery
Its spell shall cast,
Wherever leaf may grow, wherever tide may flow,
Till all be past.
O secret queen of power, at this enchanted hour
We ask your boon.
May fortune's favour fall upon true witches all,
O Lady Moon.[31]

Drawing Down the Moon

One of the better examples of the moon being associated with the powers of witchcraft comes from ancient Greece, where the feared witches of the northeastern pastoral region of Thessaly were said to draw their power from the moon, which they could command and bring down from the sky. Both Sophocles and Aristophanes wrote about the Thessalian witches in the 5th century BCE, and Plato wrote about them a century later. Horace, Virgil, Ovid and Lucan further hailed the moon-drawing charm at the turn of the Common Era. In the 17th century, Englishman John Dryden described a heroine whose 'eyes have power beyond Thessalian charms to drawn the moon from heaven'.

How the Thessalian witches drew down the moon's power is not 100% certain. However, a vase allegedly dating back to the 2nd century BCE depicted two Thessalian witches drawing down the moon's power through the use of their swords, whereby they would capture the image of the moon on a blade, which was then used to put a person into a light trance. This image has captured the imagination of writers for centuries, right up until the modern era, when German classical scholar Wilhelm Heinrich Roscher (1884–1937) produced a line drawing of the vase's image. Although the whereabouts of the original Greek vase is today unknown, Roscher's drawing depicts two witches allegedly calling upon the power of the full moon. Little wonder, therefore, that the witches of Thessaly were feared, so much so that in the 1st century CE Roman poet Publius Papinius Statius in *Thebaid* 3.558–9 referred to 'Drawing Down the Moon' as 'the Thessalian crime':

Figure 7: Hamilton, William, and Johann Heinrich Wilhelm Tischbein. Collection of Engravings from Ancient Vases... Naples: W. Tischbein, 1791. Department of Special Collections, Bryn Mawr College Libraries.

It is drawn down for the purpose of erotic attraction magic.
It is either made to turn pale, or blood red when subjected to drawing.
The drawing down can be counteracted by the clashing of bronze cymbals.
When brought down to the earth it deposits its foam on plants as 'moon juice' (virus lunarae). This can then be collected and used in a love potion.
The control of the moon in this way is sometimes contextualised against the witches' wider ability to control the sun and stars and consequently time itself.

The Thessalian women pay a terrible price for drawing down of the moon: they must lose either children or an eye.[32]

No one knows for sure where Statius got the idea that the moon could be drawn down from the sky; however, around the same time, Plutarch hinted in his work that this may have been the way of thinking with respect to lunar eclipses, and therefore, many may have adapted this belief. During a full lunar eclipse, the moon certainly does appear to turn blood red because it reflects only the sunlight refracted red through Earth's atmosphere. The Roman poet, Ovid, certainly described the moon as such in his first book, *Amores* (the Loves), at 2.1.23–8:

Incantations draw down the horns of the bloody moon and call back the snowy horses of the departing sun. By an incantation, snakes are burst and their jaws broken off, and waters turn around and flow back to their sources. Doors have yielded before incantations, and the bar, fixed into the post, has been overcome by an incantation, though made of oak.[33]

Within contemporary witchcraft, the 'Drawing Down the Moon' rite is often considered central. During this rite, which usually takes place during the time of the full moon, the High Priestess of the coven becomes the goddess incarnate by entering a trance state through which the High Priest invokes the spirit of the goddess to enter her body and speak through her. If this is not able to occur, the High Priestess may recite a more formal dramatic dialogue, such as the 'Charge of the Goddess', written by the aforementioned Doreen Valiente. This beautiful piece was inspired from an invocation found in *Aradia, or the Gospel of the Witches*, published in 1899 by US folklorist, Charles Godfrey Leland, which he believed to be the religious text from a group of witches located in Tuscany, Italy.

Within the first chapter, entitled 'How Diana Gave Birth to

Aradia', Aradia is the daughter of the goddess Diana. Aradia
was sent to Earth to teach people witchcraft and ensure that
they continued to worship her mother. At the end of the chapter,
Aradia instructs the people:

> When I shall have departed from this world,
> Whenever ye have need of anything,
> Once in the month, and when the moon is full,
> Ye shall assemble in some desert place,
> Or in a forest all together join
> To adore the potent spirit of your queen,
> My mother, great Diana. She who fain
> Would learn all sorcery yet has not won
> Its deepest secrets, them my mother will
> Teach her, in truth all things as yet unknown.[34]

While the authenticity of *Aradia, or the Gospel of the Witches* has
always been questioned, Professor Ronald Hutton[35] presents
three theories in his scholarly study of the roots of neo-paganism,
which included that it was a genuine text of an underground
Italian religion; that Maddelena, who gave the text to Leland,
wrote it based on her own family tradition; or finally, that Leland
forged the text. Regardless of what the truth is behind Leland's
book, the 'Charge of the Goddess' continues to be 'one of the
most serious and beautiful in the modern Craft'.[36]

Along a similar theme to that of 'Drawing Down the Moon',
US author Elizabeth Pepper describes a more personal rite that she
states is closer to original sorcery as recorded by Publius Papinius
Statius than contemporary witchcraft, 'its purpose being to renew
psychic energy, increase divinatory perception and to capture the
elusive fifth element – the quintessence to nourish the soul'.[37]

Pepper suggests using a bowl of water to 'capture the moon's
reflection'. When this has been achieved, stare at the image and
slowly count silently to nine. Close your eyes and while holding

the visualisation of the moon in your mind, drink the water from the bowl.

This exercise may have been a forerunner to the now popular exercise for modern witches and pagan of gathering moon water when they fill a glass jar with spring or filtered water and leave it out under the moonlight to 'charge'. The water is then used in rituals and sacred ceremonies over the following month.

Scrying with the Moon

Scrying is the ancient art of divination by concentrating on a smooth and shiny surface until clairvoyant visions appear. The term 'scrying' comes from the English word 'descry', meaning 'to make out dimly' or 'to reveal'. The most familiar image of the scryer is the gypsy woman hunched over a crystal ball. Other ways to scry are to use the moon or a lunar image. In ancient times, scryers gazed into the still water of a lake or pond at night. Their powers were enhanced if the light of the moon, especially at full moon, fell upon the water. The same procedure is used today.

Unscrupulous scryers used a trick said to have been invented by Pythagoras. They wrote a message in blood on a looking glass in advance, then stood behind their client and turned the glass toward the moon. The client was then invited to read the message on the moon reflected in the mirror as though it were written on the moon itself – a divine revelation.

The *Egyptian Book of the Dead* contains various references to the magic mirror of the goddess Hathor being used to see the future. In the 16th century, French astrologer Nostradamus made notes about staring into a bowl of water by candlelight to gain inspiration.

Within English folklore can be found a way to reveal when a person will marry through the act of scrying. During a full moon, a person should go to a stream, or any other body of flowing water, and hold a silk square over the water with the moon behind them. The silk will cause several reflections of the moon to be cast on the water. The number of reflections is the number of months before the person will marry.

Another scrying method occurs during the night of the full moon. Pour some water into a bowl and position yourself so that you can see the moon's light reflected directly in the water. As you stare into the water, relax your eyes and take note of any patterns, symbols or pictures that you may see. Also take note of any thoughts or words that spontaneously enter your mind, as well as any sensations that you may feel. It is recommended to write everything down, even if it does not make sense at the time.

The length of time that you perform this exercise will depend on you. It may be just a few minutes, or even an hour. When you find yourself starting to become restless or being distracted by mundane thoughts, then it is best to stop. The water can be left out overnight to further charge it or it can be tipped into the garden (or over a pot plant) as an offering.

To charge an object by the moon, take a small round mirror and place it on the palm of your hand. Set the object to be charged upon the mirror, and hold it out at about eye level as you face the moon. Looking toward the moon, squint your eyes until it appears that you can see three beams emanating from the moon. With your right hand, throw three kisses to each aspect of Lady Lunar, saying:

O Lady Lunar of the midnight skies
Whose beauty fills the heavens on high
Hear my words as I stand before thee
Seeking your blessings to shine upon me.
I beseech thee, O Lady Lunar, whose wisdom is true
Teach me of thine mysteries as I worship you.
Speak to my spirit as my body rests at night
Shield me from oppressors, and grant me the sight.
O glorious Lady Lunar of the midnight skies
Accept my praises that I offer on high.
Let thy glory shine about me.
O gracious Queen of Heaven, so blessed be.[38]

Lunar Incenses and Oils

The sense of smell can heighten your connection with the moon through the crafting of incenses and oils. Near my ritual circle, I have an old wisteria tree growing. While in full flower during early spring, the delicate scent of the flowers invokes many pleasant memories of the evening breeze when I have been outside watching the moon. Likewise, both jasmine and gardenia are associated with the moon.

To capture that delicate lunar essence, a very simple recipe for a lunar incense can be made by mixing together two parts frankincense with one part sandalwood. Wicca author Scott Cunningham[39] suggests mixing together four parts[40] frankincense, three parts myrrh, two parts benzoin, one part each of gardenia petals and sandalwood and a half part each of orris root, thyme, poppy seeds and rose petals.

Other suitable incense recipes that can be used during a lunar rite are:

- Two parts each of juniper berries and myrrh, one part each of rose petals, and mugwort and a half part of marigold petals. One part of sandalwood powder can also be added to this recipe.
- Two parts each of sandalwood and frankincense, a half part of gardenia petals, and a quarter part of rose petals.

When used in incenses, almond, jasmine, sandalwood and myrrh also possess the ability to trigger our olfactory receptors which aid in heightening our perception, intuition and psychism. This in turn can enhance our magical workings, as well as when we undertake meditations, pathworkings and even shamanic journeys.

These incense blends made from resins and botanicals can be stored in jars or ziplock bags, and are to be burned over charcoal discs, which can be purchased from Middle Eastern supermarkets, esoteric shops, some health food stores or online stores such as my own LunaNoire Creations.

Lunar Oils

You can also make your own anointing oil, which may be more practical to use during moon rituals and lunar magical workings. It is essential that you use a reputable brand of essential oils as opposed to fragrant oils, especially if you wish to use these oils on your skin.

When I undertook my aromatherapy training back in the mid-1990s, I was told that no essential oil should be ingested and the only essential oils that should be applied neat (undiluted) directly to the skin are tea tree (*Melaleuca alternifolia*), provided that it has not oxidised, lavender (*Lavandula angustifolia*), Roman chamomile (Chamaemelum nobile), rose (Rosa damascene), sandalwood (*Santalum album* or *Santalum spicatum*), cypress (*Cupressus sempervirens*), eucalyptus (*Eucalyptus radiate* or *globulus*) and Bay Laurel (*Laurus nobilis*), and even then only in extremely small amounts (e.g. one or two drops and after a test patch has been undertaken). Today, however, I notice a number of brands insist that all of their essential oils are safe not only to be applied neat to any skin but also to ingest. This contradicts what I was told, so I would recommend you undertake your own research, especially when it comes to ingesting essential oils. Further, bear in mind that depending on the sensitivity of your skin, you may find that you react even to the 'safer' oils. For this reason, I personally prefer to dilute my essential oils in a base or carrier oil such as jojoba, almond, extra virgin or coconut oil.

When making your own oils, it is recommended to use no more than 10 drops of essential oil to 10 ml of your chosen base oil. You are after quality, not quantity; all you need do with the oil is to put a few drops of it on your pulse points prior to undertaking your lunar ritual or spell work. Storing your blended oils is just as important as storing your essential oil bottles. Ensure that your oils are stored out of direct sunlight, and preferably in an amber or dark glass bottle.

A final point I would mention is that if your bottle of essential oil does not come with a dropper in its cap, you can purchase glass droppers from a chemist or health store. That way, you can accurately measure the essential oil drops.

Recipes of Lunar Oil Blends

The following oil blends can be mixed and placed straight into an oil diffuser or oil burner. If you are intending to apply the oils to your skin, as mentioned above, mix the oils in 10 ml of a base or carrier oil:

- **New Moon:** Mix together three drops of tangerine essential oil and two drops each of lemon and frankincense essential oil to allow space for any new creative ideas that arise. Alternatively, two drops each of lavender, clary sage and jasmine essential oils will help your mind to settle, which will in turn allow more creative insights to appear.
- **Waxing Crescent:** Mix together three drops of sweet orange essential oil, two drops of cedarwood and one drop of cypress essential oil for courage in focusing on your desires.
- **First Quarter:** Mix together three drops of rose essential oil, two drops of patchouli and one drop of lemon essential oil to help encourage feelings of focus while also releasing any tension.
- **Gibbous Moon:** Mix together three drops each of rosemary and lemon essential oil to encourage forging ahead with your goals.
- **Full Moon:** Mix together two drops each of sweet orange, geranium and ylang ylang essential oil for balance. If you need assistance in releasing difficult emotions, try mixing together two drops each of rose and bergamot and one drop of patchouli essential oil.

- **Disseminating/Waning Crescent**: Mix together three drops of rose essential oil and two drops each of geranium and lavender essential oil to encourage acceptance and relaxation. If you find that you need a deeper level of relaxation, then you might like to mix together two drops each of jasmine, lavender and ylang ylang essential oil.
- **Last Quarter**: Mix together three drops each of grapefruit and juniper berry essential oil, with one drop of vetiver essential oil to encourage releasing and letting go of thoughts and actions in a more decisive way.
- **Balsamic Moon**: Mix together two drops each of frankincense, myrrh and sweet orange essential oils to help ground you into the present so that you are able to surrender more easily. Another blend that you might like to try is eight drops of cedarwood and two drops each of cinnamon clary sage and orange essential oil.
- **Dark Moon**: Mix together eight drops of lavender, three drops of rosemary and two drops each of fennel and lemon essential oil for you to go completely within.

The more you familiarise yourself with essential oils and their aromas, the more you may like to experiment with the different scents and notes to create your own unique oil blends.

Lunar Healing

Endymion the shepherd, as his flock he guarded,
She, the Moon, Selene, saw him, loved him, sought him.
Coming down from heaven to the glade on Latmus,
Kissed him, lay beside him.
Blessed is his fortune. Evermore he slumbers,
Tossing not nor turning, Endymion the shepherd.
('Myth about Selene' by 3rd century Greek poet, Theocritus)

Our ancestors believed that the moon was a powerful force, and they often held ceremonies and prepared medicinal potions and other concoctions based upon the various phases. The new moon offered a new 'seeding' energy, whereas the full was for the harvest. The time between the new and the full (when the moon is waxing) would 'draw', or increase, the potency of something, and the time between the full and the new (when the moon is waning) could reduce, or 'pull out'. For example, to make a cleansing concoction, this would be prepared between the full moon and new moon phases because the mixture would carry the potency of the reduction. If the concoction was to build a system up, preparation would be made from the new moon to the full.

According to the *Farmer's Almanac*, people who believe in the power of the moon also consider dental care and elective surgery unwise around the times of the full moon because of the risk of increased bleeding, as even doctors attending to the wounded during the US Civil War noted.

A study of acute aortic dissection repair performed through the Cardiovascular Institute at Rhode Island in the United States found a lunar impact on recovery from cardiovascular surgery. The study reported a reduction in death rates during a waning moon and shorter stays in the hospital by up to four days during a full moon.

It has been suggested that lower death rates occur during a waning moon because the patient is responding to the age-old theory that the toxicity is 'drawn' out at that time, to keep their strength for recovery. The shorter hospital stays during a full moon could indicate that the higher availability of energy in the atmosphere around the full moon contributes to feeding the vital essence in the body of those who might otherwise be weak, thus enabling quicker recovery and release from hospital care.

When working with the moon for health and healing, similar principles apply to those when working magic:

- **Waxing Crescent**: A time for growth and expansion. This is a time for 'new beginnings' – a time to increase expansion in life and focus on intentions related to abundance. Put yourself out there (socially, romantically, in your career, etc.), take the time to expand your mind through learning and trying new things. Step outside your comfort zone and take a risk. Create space in your life to welcome unexpected surprises from the universe. Nurture your health with nutritious foods and drink more water.
- **First Quarter**: A time to refocus. The seeds you planted are beginning to come to fruition, and you begin to take root and feel your inner power. Capitalise on your determination and stay focused on intentions, even re-evaluating your direction as you move forward.
- **Waxing Gibbous**: A time for attainment. Your 'seeds' begin to blossom; this represents a time of gaining and attainment. Relax and enjoy the fruits of your labour after you have achieved your dreams.
- **Full Moon**: A time to shine. The 'seeds' are in full bloom. This is an opportunity to take in the power of the full moon. This period represents transformation, fertility and completion. Meditation and healing take place at the fullest level during this phase of the moon. Avoid tensions and strong emotional reactions. Focus on healing energy to calm intense thoughts and feelings.
- **Disseminating**: A time for release. The waning phase of the moon begins, as does its energy. It is time to reduce bad habits and negative thinking. Also called the 'disseminating moon', this marks a phase for closing chapters and completion.
- **Last Quarter**: A time for reflection. This is a time of contemplation and reflection upon the progress made over the past month. Consider your achievements and where you would like to move forward for growth during

the next phase of your goals.

- **Balsamic:** A time to rest. The moon only appears partially illuminated in the sky just before the formation of the new moon; harness the waning crescent moon energy by taking this as a moment to heal and rest as you prepare for the next phase of the moon.

An additional rule of thumb is that the time during the waxing phases of the moon can be used for regenerating, absorbing and supplying. Focus on building up and strengthening your body and its organs. Because the body absorbs more easily, it may put on more weight easily with the same amount of food. Certain minerals, such as magnesium, calcium and iron, are also more readily absorbed during the waxing moon. During the waning phases, however, the focus should be placed on detoxifying and washing out, sweating out and even breathing out. Drinking a detoxification tea, such as nettle, during spring has strong preventative and purifying effects that are believed to last the whole year. Some people also recommend fasting at the new moon because this is said to prevent illnesses. I would recommend having a discussion with your medical practitioner before undertaking any such processes, especially if you have underlying health issues.

Lunar Personalities

Just as the sun can characterise different traits depending on what astrological sign it is in, so too does the moon – Lady Lunar influences our moods and the tone of the day. As mentioned in Part II, the moon enters each sign of the astrological system and stays there for up to 2.5 days. When the full moon enters each astrological sign, it can highlight areas in our life that are either overemphasised or underemphasised. It can also affect our moons and our mental health.

The following list relates to the general energetic mood when the moon moves into the different astrological signs. I have also provided things that you might like to consider when working with these differing astrological moons, recording your discoveries in your lunar journal:

- **Moon in Aries** ♈: This is the time to ask yourself whether you have been hot-headed, selfish or argumentative. Are you being too impulsive, blunt or uncompassionate? Are you ignoring the sensitivities of other people?
- **Moon in Taurus** ♉: This is the time to ask yourself whether you have been lazy, overly self-indulgent, obsessive with money or status, stubborn or jealous. Are you getting enough exercise?
- **Moon in Gemini** ♊: This is the time to ask yourself whether you have been too gossipy or superficial, glossing over the feelings of other people or changing your mind too quickly. Have you done enough reading to expand your knowledge?
- **Moon in Cancer** ♋: This is the time to ask yourself whether you have been feeling insecure, moody or manipulative, taking issues head on or moving sidewards around them. Are you being secretive or paranoid, spending enough time with family or those people who you may consider to be like family?
- **Moon in Leo** ♌: This is the time to ask yourself whether you have been too self-centred, egotistical or arrogant or treating those around you with less respect. Are you showing yourself enough love?
- **Moon in Virgo** ♍: This is the time to ask yourself whether you have been too prickly, pedantic or critical of yourself or of other people. Are you worrying about things, attracting negativity, complaining too much? Do you pay enough attention to the details you need?
- **Moon in Libra** ♎: This is the time to ask yourself whether you have been too concerned about your general

appearance, too easily influenced by others or gullible, living your life through other people. Do you spend enough time on your beauty?

- **Moon in Scorpio** ♏: This is the time to ask yourself whether you have been jealous, vengeful, suspicious or focusing on the negative as opposed to the positive. Are you getting enough sex or intimacy to feel good about yourself?
- **Moon in Sagittarius** ♐: This is the time to ask yourself whether you have been too flippant or carefree, irresponsible, distracted, overconfident or avoiding situations and or people. Have you been seeing the bigger picture or solely focusing on the immediate situations?
- **Moon in Capricorn** ♑: This is the time to ask yourself whether you have been ambitious to the point of being ruthless, hard-headed and obsessed with work. Have you been planning all aspects of your life enough or too much?
- **Moon in Aquarius** ♒: This is the time to ask yourself whether you have been too pragmatic, being in your head too much as opposed to in your heart, trying too hard to make friends. Have you allowed yourself to move forwards?
- **Moon in Pisces** ♓: This is the time to ask yourself whether you have been overly sensitive or too dreamy, acting as a martyr or being easily led. Have you been in touch with your intuitive side, following dreams and hunches?

Anatomy by the Moon

According to renowned herbalist Paul Beyerl, the moon corresponds and governs much of the brain and the rear pituitary, the left eye and the digestive system (oesophagus, stomach and hormones associated with the alimentary system) as well as the uterus, breasts, ovaries and menstrual cycle in women. Most modern medical astrologers place the lymphatic system and the sympathetic system under the governance of the moon as well.

Within Chinese medicine, astrology is used to map and observe a patient's illness. In particular, the progression of the moon is used. Some imbalances within our bodies, such as colds, are believed to arise when we are more vulnerable owing to emotional stress or anxieties that threaten the health of our unconscious. When working with the moon, especially with respect to your health, you might like to start paying attention to whether any patterns coincide with the lunar cycles. To do this, you will need to learn where your natal moon is located within your birth chart. This can be obtained through an astrologer or by using a number of free websites such as Astrodienst, as mentioned previously.

Once you have discovered what sign the moon was in at the time of your birth, you will be able to see if this affects you and, in particular, your health, throughout the lunar cycles. The more that you work with the lunar energies, especially on a deeper and more personal level, the deeper you go into understanding your own self through the revealing of hormonal fluctuations and possible changes in moods, eating patterns and even thought patterns.

Since the moon governs the watery tides, there are a number of herbs and planets that regulate fluidity issues generally and act upon water and blood. Cucumber helps eliminate excess water from the body and is an anti-constipatory diuretic, particularly effective in dissolving uric acid accumulations such as kidney stones. Fennel and lily are both eliminatives, laxatives and diuretics. While lily acts as a digestive antispasmodic, fennel is commonly used to stimulate the flow of milk in nursing mothers. Mugwort (*Artemisia vulgaris*) is particularly apt in its lunar attribution in that in addition to its digestive and purgative qualities, a decoction can be used quite effectively to regulate the flow of menstrual blood.

Several lunar herbs act on other fluids of the body, generally to eliminate excess and act as digestives. Camphor (*Cinnamomum camphora*) reduces fluid accumulation in the lungs and pleural sac, and therefore, offers an excellent remedy for whooping cough and pleurisy. Bitter almond (*Prunus amygdalus* var. *amara*) is used as a cough remedy and sweet almond (*Prunus dulcis* var. *dulcis*) can be used internally as a soothing syrup and externally as an emollient. Meanwhile, white sandalwood is used to reduce inflammation of mucosal tissue and is a diuretic – a decoction of the wood can further be used for indigestion.

Myrrh and sandalwood both have astringent and stomachic properties, and along with jasmine (*Jasminum officinale*) and bitter almond, have qualities ascribed to the moon that surpass those for medical uses. Bitter almond and jasmine have sedative effects; they can calm the nerves and allow a more intuitive, psychic lunar mode of brain function to manifest. It is probably also this aspect that has earned jasmine the reputation of being erotogenic, the resultant intuitive empathy accredited with aphrodisiacal properties and the ability to overcome inhibition.

When it comes to herbal concoctions, again, I strongly recommend discussing their use with your medical doctor or healthcare professional. Also, it is important to ensure that the ingredients are obtained from reputable sources or made by a properly trained herbalist or naturopath.

The Moon and Emotions

Lunar energy can potentially affect your emotions, your mental state and your body's own natural rhythms, even more so if you are a woman. However, men can notice this effect as well, especially when they become more attuned to their bodies. When you consciously decide to tune into the phases of the moon, you can use it as a bridge to bring a deeper awareness of your connection with the universe and beyond. This enables you to become more consciously aware of how the moon's energy affects and relates to your mind, body and soul.

There are no right or wrong answers to the following prompts. They can assist you in gaining a deeper connection with the moon. You might like to record your responses to any of the following wherever appropriate in your lunar journal to see whether it contains any consistencies as your lunar awareness grows:

- **Your menstrual cycle:** If you are a bleeding woman, does your monthly bleeding coincide with specific phases of the moon? Many women find that they bleed during the darker phase or the full moon. This is covered in more detail in the next section.

- **Your energy:** Do you find that you are more energetic during certain phases of the moon than others? Knowing ahead of time how your own personal energy fluctuates can help you anticipate periods of productivity and planned rest.

- **Your moods:** While the moon may not affect our emotions to the degree that other cycles do (e.g. a woman's menstrual cycle), it is still worth noting whether your moods ebb and flow with the differing phases of the moon. This can be beneficial even if you do not have a menstrual cycle.

- **Your results:** Have you ever noticed that you tend to have an onslaught of new ideas during one certain phase of a moon over the others? Or do you have new ideas that you are more likely to effectively act on during one phase more than at any other time? If so, does this coincide with the waxing phases of the moon?

Women and the Moon

The moon's influence can readily be observed in a woman's menstrual cycle. There is no coincidence that the length of the average menstrual cycle is around 28 to 29.5 days, the length of time the moon takes to move through all of its phases. Since ancient times, many cultures have referred to women having their menstrual periods as being 'on their moon'. The menstrual blood is often referred to as 'moon blood' or a woman being on her 'moon time'.

The menstrual cycle governs the flow not only of fluids but also of information and creativity. Many women find they are at peak expression in the outer world during the first half of their cycles until ovulation (coinciding with the waxing to full moon). During this time, not only do women's bodies secrete hormones associated with sexual attractiveness to others but women are naturally more receptive during this time, including to new ideas.

The last few days of the waning moon and leading up to the new moon tends to be the time for reflection and identifying what needs to be changed in one's life. During this phase of the moon, the veils between the worlds of the seen and unseen, the conscious and the unconscious, are at their thinnest. That is why during menstruation (as well as pregnancy and menopause), our emotions and perceptions are heightened, and we are most in tune with our inner knowing.

One interesting thing about connection between the moon and the menstrual cycle is that, even in modern times when many women are not connected to the lunar cycles, they still experience the effect of the moon to some degree. For example, when women live together, their ovulations and menstruation tend to be in sync. This is why women living in the same household or boarding school dormitories will often menstruate at the same time. Women who work together can experience this as well.

If you are a menstruating woman, plotting your menstrual cycle when you are not using contraception, such as the pill, can be a rather rewarding process and provide a deeper insight into your own ebbing and flowing nature. I have provided a chart that can be used for this at the end of this section. For non-menstruating women and men, this chart can also be used to track other aspects of their lives throughout the lunar cycle, such as energy levels and emotions.

A Moon Chart

Since the moon cycles affect each of us on different levels, using a moon chart helps us notice these effects. If you do not have a moon diary, you might like to make copies of the chart that appears on the following page because this will enable you to track your lunar influences over the next few months.

Begin by discovering what phase the moon is in during its cycle and write the appropriate date on your chart before completing the rest of the chart.

What you track is completely up to you. It is ideal to first track any overt physical changes you experience each month. For women who are menstruating, track your bleeding days in the first row of the chart. If you are breastfeeding, track that towards the top. Track your usual monthly symptoms, from PMS to cramps to acne to breast sensitivity. Other suggestions on what to track (which can be used by men and non-menstruating women) include moods, cravings, appetite, diet change, energy levels, sexual arousal, dreams, psychic ability and intuition, spaceyness, inspiration and which astrological sign the moon is passing through.

You may wish to colour code or draw specific images or even emojis to indicate your modes, emotions, thoughts, energy levels and so on.

You may want to use + and − signs, check marks and one-word responses in the blanks. The main guideline here is to keep it simple. Place your chart somewhere you will see it every day, but where it will still be private – perhaps in your personal journal or in a book you are reading, or perhaps taped to the inside of a wardrobe door. It does not take much energy to maintain this chart because you only need to pay attention to the items you are tracking and to note any noticeable changes.

In addition to maintaining a chart, try to observe the moon more often. Begin becoming more conscious of her influence on your body and your life. The rewards of exploring our connection to the moon can be enormous! Invite her to shine her silvery light on you.

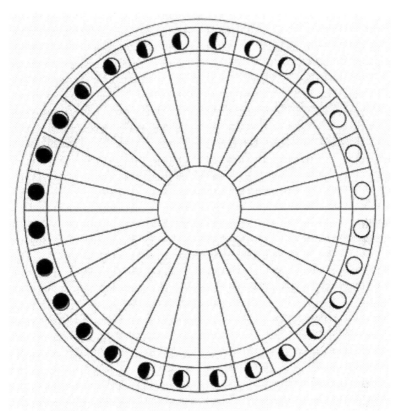

Figure 8: Moon Chart

Working Magic During an Eclipse

It sounded as if the Streets were running
And then - the Streets stood still -
Eclipse - was all we could see at the Window
And Awe - was all we could feel.

By and by - the boldest stole out of his Covert
To see if Time was there -
Nature was in an Opal Apron,
Mixing fresher Air.
(From *Poems & Letters* by Emily Dickinson)

As we observed in Part II, both solar and lunar eclipses can have specific effects on our wellbeing. They bring about a change in energies that tend to put us where we need to be, especially on a deeper, soul level, and have been described as "portals of transformation" in that they can remove stagnation from our lives and allow space for much needed spiritual growth to occur. It is not uncommon to feel the energy of eclipses as early as a month prior and for it to last some six months later. The energies of an eclipse often affect the magic we undertake.

Within occult texts, a solar eclipse is often described as the 'alchemical wedding' in which the sun marries the moon, creating a perfect balance. As such, within various magical traditions, the eclipse is often considered one of the more powerful times to work magic, with both the energies of the solar and lunar eclipses being distinctively different.

The energy of the solar eclipse is considered similar to that of a powerful moon, when important beginnings or endings occur. It is the perfect time to work magic that relates to releasing outdated thought patterns and ideas that are holding you back. The energy generated by a solar eclipse provides you with the power to break free from or release previous restrictions as well as a confidence boost to completely transform into a new form. In other words, magic associated with a solar eclipse can be viewed as 'metamorphosis', the time to transcend to a new state of being. Some astrologers consider that the solar eclipse is linked to destiny related to your broader journey to higher consciousness.

As mentioned previously, solar eclipses always occur at the new moon. The new moon has a solar, or yang, energy. This is why new moons are associated with new beginnings. Conversely, full moons are associated with culminations and have a yin energy, making things happen and feeling 'fated'.

If a solar eclipse challenges your logic and your authority in your life, then a lunar eclipse will challenge your emotional readiness for a change. The energy of a lunar eclipse, which always occur at the full moon, encourages you to face your own insecurities. In doing this, you not only gain the ability to imagine that a change can occur and what this change will bring but also ensure that you have the willpower.

A lunar eclipse, therefore, is the perfect time to face the past and discover the roots of any fears or insecurities, how they are linked to you, your emotions and your current state of being. It is often recommended that such workings are done with the guidance of spiritual guides (including guardian angels), the gods or your own higher self or higher consciousness. During a lunar eclipse, it is also perfect timing to contact the 'other worlds' and 'other states of being'.

The lunar eclipse can offer the perfect time to consider what you want to have brought from the shadows into the light. Just prior to the eclipse, consider the following and write your thoughts in your lunar journal:

- What dreams or goals do you have that need to be infused with new energy?
- Are there any unresolved hurts or emotional wounds that need to be let go of once and for all, any resentment to be removed from your life?
- Is there a secret, an underlying message or even a plan that needs to be exposed?

Lunar eclipses occur two weeks prior to the solar eclipse. Meditate on the lunar eclipse to face your inhibitions. These then can be released during the following solar eclipse.

If you want to tap into the energy of the lunar eclipse, it is essential that you plan your magical working around the exact timing of the passing shadow. When the moon is in the full lunar eclipse, treat these few moments as if the moon were in the dark phase. Ensure your intentions are clear, especially if you wish to expose some wrongdoing.

It is important that you all your facts are 100% true and accurate. Further, it is important that you are not acting from ego or vengeance. Consider the repercussions. As I mentioned in my previous book, *Contemporary Witchcraft: Foundational Practices for a Magical Life*, when performing acts of magic, being able to take full responsibility for our actions is always the key. You are working magic after all – magic causes change to occur and this change may not always be how we envisage it. Magic is a game. It comes with power and responsibility. At the end of the day, if you are not able to take responsibility for your magic, then maybe you should reconsider whether you should be using it after all.

Kamea of the Moon

A *kamea*, or a magic square, is a representation of spiritual forces connected with a particular cosmic body. It uses a mathematical format in which the squares are arranged in such a way that any row is equal to the sum of any column. While the creation of kameas uses magical techniques that are more commonly associated with high magic as opposed to contemporary witchcraft, they can be used to heighten magical workings, especially when working with the seven classical planetary bodies (the sun, the moon, Mercury, Venus, Mars, Jupiter and Saturn). While a kamea sets the specific planetary forces in motion, there is also a correspondence seal that brings a halt to such forces. Each planetary kamea also has an 'intelligence', which is perceived as an evolutionary, guiding or inspiring entity. There is also a 'spirit', considered more of a neutral force. For the purpose of this book, we will be addressing the Kamea of the Moon as a matrix for lunar energy.

The Kamea of the Moon consists of nine squares containing 81 numbers that total 3,321. Nine is the number associated with the moon within a number of magical and esoteric systems. According to German occult writer Heinrich Cornelius Agrippa von Nettesheim, 'it renders the bearer grateful, amiable, pleasant, cheerful, honoured, removing all malice and ill will'.[41] It also offers security when travelling, increases wealth and health in the body, and drives away enemies and other 'evil things', especially if the kamea is engraved in silver. However, if it is engraved in lead and burned, it will make that place unfortunate, as well as the inhabitants. In other words, it can attract much misfortune.

The most common use of kameas is to connect with that particular planetary power, in this case, the moon. If you trace a sigil (an image) made from converting the letters of your name, or desire, into numbers onto the kamea, you begin to instil the force behind the magical field of that planet into your own aura. The sigil can then be used on its own or kept on the kamea, which was traditionally made into a talisman out of the corresponding metal for that planet. As mentioned above, in the case of a Kamea of the Moon, that metal would be silver. Today, not everyone is able to afford silver (or gold, which is the corresponding metal for the sun), so more practical alternatives would be to use silver paper or cardboard, or a pen with silver ink.

While you do not have to be well versed in high magic or the Qabalah to construct kameas, if you are interested in exploring this magical technique beyond what I cover in this book, then I suggest that you consider studying these styles of magic. I do consider it important that you understand what that particular planet governs. The following correspondences can be considered when designing your lunar kamea:

- **Influences:** Astral travel, birth and reincarnation, clairvoyance, dreams, emotions, fertility, imagination, nursing, receptivity, the unconscious, trade and commerce, and for women in general
- **Day of the week:** Monday
- **Element:** Water
- **Colour:** Silver, white, light purple
- **Metal:** Silver

- **Astrological sign:** Cancer
- **Crystals:** Aquamarine, moonstone, pearl
- **Botanicals:** Camphor, jasmine, lotus, orris root, sandalwood, star anise
- **Spirit:** Chasmodai

Begin making your Kamea of the Moon by drawing a grid that has nine rows and nine columns. The numbering of each of the boxes with the sequence is provided below. Some magical traditions advise that you should start with 1 and continue filling the boxes in numerological order until you reach the last number. You may wish to follow this or complete the numbering of the squares according to whatever method resonates with you.

37	78	29	70	21	62	13	54	5
6	38	79	30	71	22	63	14	46
47	7	39	80	31	72	23	55	15
16	48	8	40	81	32	64	24	56
57	17	49	9	41	73	33	65	25
26	58	18	50	1	42	74	34	66
67	37	59	10	51	2	43	75	35
36	68	19	60	11	52	3	44	76
77	28	69	20	61	12	53	4	45

Figure 9: Kamea of the Moon

As mentioned previously, if making your kamea out of silver is beyond your financial means, use the above colour correspondences and a light purple pen on silver paper or a silver marker on white paper, for example.

The next step is to use a form of numerology to transform your name or desire into a series of numbers. Traditionally, a system known as Gematria is used, which is based on the Hebrew alphabet, in which each letter equates to a specific number. However, the following Pythagorean or Western system, which is found within modern numerology (based on the numbers 1 to 9) can also be used, as follows:

1	2	3	4	5	6	7	8	9
A	B	C	D	E	F	G	H	I
J	K	L	M	N	O	P	Q	R
S	T	U	V	W	X	Y	Z	

Figure 10: Pythagorean Table

As an example of the Pythagorean method, the numerical values for the letters of my name are F = 6, R = 9, A = 1, N = 5, C = 3, E = 5 and S = 1. When you commence drawing your sigil, mark the starting point with a small circle, and when you finish, mark where you end with a line – a tail. In the following sigil created using my name, you will see that I have also included a small loop through which the line doubles back to the number 5:

37	78	29	70	21	62	13	54	5
6	38	79	30	71	22	63	14	46
47	7	39	80	31	72	23	55	15
16	48	8	40	81	32	64	24	56
57	17	49	9	41	73	33	65	25
26	58	18	50	1	42		34	66
67	37	59	10	51	2	43	75	35
36	68	19	60	11	52	3	44	76
77	28	69	20	61	12	53	4	45

Figure 11: Kamea of the Moon for my name

To further enhance the power of your kamea, you could construct it on a Monday (the day of the week named after and ruled by the moon). There are other observances you might like to consider, including the use of planetary hours. However, there is not room in this book to go into detail, so I would recommend investigating high magic.

When your sigil is created, you can turn it into a talisman by drawing the following Seal of the Moon on the other side of your square.

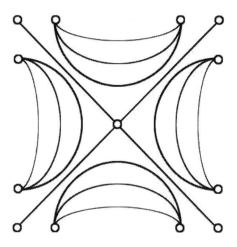

Figure 12: The Seal of the Moon

The next step is to consecrate and empower your completed Kamea of the Moon by passing it through incense smoke. Alternatively, you can use the charging ritual that is given in the next section. Your kamea can also be anointed with a blessing oil before ensuring that you carry it with you or if your kamea is to assist you to remember your dreams, for example, then keep it under your pillow.

For the second example of constructing a kamea, I will use the English alphabet gematria created by Agrippa, which includes the obsolete letter 'Hi', to create a sigil for 'dream recall':

A	B	C	D	E	F	G	H	I
1	2	3	4	5	6	7	8	9
K	L	M	N	O	P	Q	R	S
10	20	30	40	50	60	70	80	90
T	U	X	Y	Z	J	V	Hi	W
100	200	300	400	500	600	700	800	900

Figure 13: English Alphabet Gematria Table

Using the gematria table, the numerological value of 'dream recall' is as follows, with any number that does not appear on the kamea being reduced: D = 4, R = 80 (reduced to 8), E = 5, A = 1, M = 30 R = 80 (reduced to 8), E = 5, C = 3, A = 1, L = 20, and the final L = 20.

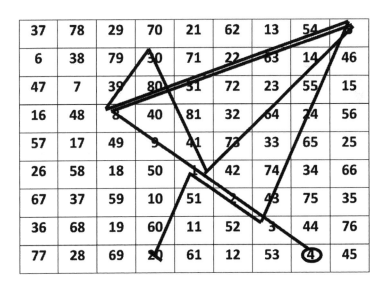

Figure 14: Kamea of the Moon for Dream Recall

Instead of creating a Kamea of the Moon for dream recall, I might like to include the sigil itself in a magical working. Therefore, on a Monday, I would take a skewer or sharp knife and carefully etch the sigil that I have created into a white or silver candle. I would then anoint the candle with sandalwood or jasmine essential oil, and meditate on my desire before I light the candle.

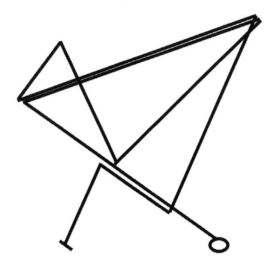

Figure 15: Sigil for Dream Recall

As the candle burns, I would then recite an appropriate chant, such as in the following example, to further enhance reaching my goal:

> *Lady Lunar, mystical light*
> *My dreams I remember here tonight*
> *With all my will and all my might*
> *I am guided by my astral sight.*

The key to making a successful talisman such as a kamea is to allow an appropriate amount of time for its completion. This is because you should be focusing solely on what you are doing (i.e. making your talisman) and adding as much of your personal energy as possible into it.

Depending on what your Kamea of the Moon, or any other

talisman you have created, is for, in some magical traditions, one way of releasing its power is to burn it, or destroy it in some way. This process can be likened to the beautiful mandalas that Buddhist monks make from carefully placing coloured sand into intricate patterns. Such mandalas can take many months to create, all the while prayers and sacred chants are recited, only to then be destroyed upon completion. It is believed that the destruction of such mandalas acts as a reminder of the impermanence of life. The coloured sand, once swept up into an urn, is then disposed of in flowing water as a way of dispersing the healing powers to the whole world.

Charging Lunar Talismans

The following is a somewhat simple technique that can be used for charging talismans and amulets, through using the full moon as well as the astrological sign that the moon is in. More information about what these astrological signs (or keys) relate to in regard to magic can be found in Part II. A quick guide is:

- Aries, Leo, Sagittarius: For works of love and friendship.
- Taurus, Virgo, Capricorn: For works of an astral nature.
- Gemini, Libra, Aquarius: For consciousness and mental powers.
- Cancer, Scorpio, Pisces: For subconscious and psychic matters.

Go outside beneath the full moon. Take a small round mirror (such as a small make-up or compact mirror) and place it on the palm of your hand. Set the object that you wish to charge upon the mirror, and hold the mirror out at about eye level as you face the moon. Looking towards the moon, squint your eyes until you can see three beams emanating from the moon. With your right hand, throw three kisses to each aspect of the goddess, saying:

Three for the Maiden (three kisses),
Three for the Crone (three kisses),
Three for the Mother (three kisses),
For the light they have shown.

Briefly state your intent, concentrating upon the bottom beams and squint slightly more so that these beams expand downwards. Do this so that the descending middle beam appears to touch the charm upon the mirror, and say:

Lady Lunar shining bright,
Send to me your blessed light
Bind my magic, bind things fast
Make my spell and desire last
Queen of Heaven hear my plead
May my will be done, so mote it be.

Close your eyes and cover the charm with your right hand. Give thanks to the moon and go into a dark room so that you can wrap the charm in a dark cloth until you need it. Do not let direct sunlight fall on it.

If you carry the charm on yourself, ensure it is hidden.

Should you encounter the person or situation for which the spell was cast, then touch the charm and say to yourself while looking at the target:

Three for the Maiden,
Three for the Crone,
Three for the Mother,
Whose target is shown.

When the next full moon appears, go out beneath her again, with your charm and your mirror. Stand with your back to the moon and hold the charm against the mirror with your thumbs.

Manipulate the mirror so that the moon appears in it. When you see the moon, say:

Three for the Maiden,
Three for the Crone,
Three for the Mother,
Return again home.

With this, if you are able to do so, fling your arms up and back so that the charm is flung up towards the moon. Leave the area without looking back. If you want the physical object back, look for it after the sun has risen.

If you are not able to do this, bury the charm either in the garden or in a pot plant. You may even like to dispose of it in your own rubbish.

The Sacred Moon Blessing Tree

The moon is no door. It is a face in its own right,
White as a knuckle and terribly upset.
It drags the sea after it like a dark crime; it is quiet
With the O-gape of complete despair. I live here.
Twice on Sunday, the bells startle the sky –
Eight great tongues affirming the Resurrection
At the end, they soberly bong out their names.
('The Moon and the Yew Tree' by Sylvia Plath)

In some traditions there is a mythical tree known as the 'Tree of the Gods', which is said to provide the fruits of immortality. The secrets of immortality are held by the moon rather than the sun because she held the power of life, death and regeneration, owing to her influence on rhythms and cycles, as well as conception and germination. Therefore, the sacred Tree of the

Gods is placed in her domain.

Past civilisations believed that the fruits of immortality grew upon this sacred tree on the moon. Ceremonies were ritually performed by Vedic priests of India, using an intoxicating milky juice extracted from the somewhat mystical soma plant (which has not been identified by modern sources). By taking soma, the priests would also be able to connect with the deeper aspects of lunar wisdom, the wisdom that comes from deep within the psyche and is innately feminine.

The highest initiation of the moon is one of wisdom that allows the psyche to influence action and to follow the inner voice. Lady Lunar, the wise mother, is beyond death and beyond the veil of illusion. She holds the secrets of feminine spirituality. Soma, the sacred liquid from the sacred moon tree, therefore, represents both immortality and profound wisdom.

While I do not have a mystical 'Tree of the Gods' in my backyard, I do have a large tree near my ritual space that I use to leave libations under and where I put my offerings from the rituals that I have undertaken. In the lower hanging branches can be found ribbons and charms, some even containing prayers and petitions that have been added to over the years – rather like the 'faery' trees or wishing trees found around the sacred wheels in Ireland and throughout the British Isles. Ensure that the material you use is 100% natural. Unfortunately, a lot of cloth these days contains polyester, which damages the environment, especially because it does not always break down properly and can easily find its way into the nests of birds.

Making a Moon Tree

You can make and decorate your own moon tree to be used on your lunar altar or as a focal point during the period coming up to and during the full moon if you do not have a physical tree yourself. For this you will need:

- a twisted branch such as from a willow tree
- silver spray paint
- a pot or container and river stones.

Spray the branch with the silver paint and leave it to dry completely. Stand the branch in the container, using the river stones to support it. Decorate your moon tree with:

- clear glass fairy Christmas lights
- any silver or clear moon or star-shaped totems or decorations
- silver or white ribbons.
- seashells, white pebbles and white paper or silk flowers.

I also like to use joss paper from Asian supermarkets, which sometimes contains a silver paper, and which breaks down into the elements. I write petitions on the pieces of joss paper that I burn as offerings or use the silver paper to create decorations.

Empower your moon tree by lighting the fairy lights (if you are using them) and two white candles at the base. Then say the following invocation:

Lady Lunar, Queen of the Night
Bless this moon tree with your sacred light
May you descend upon this tree
And bring your lunar magic here to me.

Sit quietly in meditation, opening yourself up to Lady Lunar. You might also like to write affirmations on pieces of paper and roll these into scrolls and tie them to your moon tree.

Part IV
Lunar Correspondences

A thing of beauty is a joy for ever:
Its loveliness increases; it will never
Pass into nothingness; but still will keep
A bower quiet for us, and a sleep
Full of sweet dreams, and health, and quiet breathing.
Therefore, on every morrow, are we wreathing
A flowery band to bind us to the earth,
Spite of despondence, of the inhuman dearth
Of noble natures, of the gloomy days,
Of all the unhealthy and o'er-darkened ways
Made for our searching: yes, in spite of all,
Some shape of beauty moves away the pall
From our dark spirits. Such the sun, the moon,
Trees old, and young, sprouting a shady boon
For simple sheep; and such are daffodils
With the green world they live in; and clear rills
That for themselves a cooling covert make
'Gainst the hot season; the mid-forest brake,
Rich with a sparkling of fair musk-rose blooms:
And such too is the grandeur of the dooms
We have imagined for the mighty dead;
All lovely tales that we have heard or read:
An endless fountain of immortal drink,
Pouring unto us from the heaven's brink.
(The opening lines of 'Endymion' by John Keats)

Lunar Correspondences

Folk Names of the Moon

The sun descending in the west,
The evening star does shine;
The birds are silent in their nest,
And I must seek for mine.
The moon like a flower
In heaven's high bower,
With silent delight,
Sits and smiles on the night.
('Night' by William Blake)

In earlier times, many of our ancestors tracked the changing of the seasons by following the lunar months as opposed to the solar year, on which our modern calendar is based. When European settlers arrived in America from the late 17th century onwards, they discovered that the Indigenous peoples kept track of time by both solar and lunar calendars. Each lunar month was given a name for the full moon appearing during the cycle, often reflecting seasonal conditions or activities. The European settlers adopted many of those names into their own folklore, as well as adding some of their own.

The following list contains many of these names that are circulated on social media. The main name is believed to have originated from the Algonquian peoples of Canada.[42] The subsequent names appear to have come from a number of folklore traditions that may have first been published in the Maine *Farmer's Almanac* in the 1930s. There are instances when the names are repeated for different months. The reasons for this could be numerous; the 13 lunar cycles may have been ignored, the names could have been compiled from different places where there is a change in the environment observances, or even an overlapping of moon names for that month depending on the season or elemental factors.

- **January**: Wolf Moon (the howling wolves)
  Other names: Winter Moon, Yule Moon, Old Moon, Moon of Frost in the Tepee, Cold Weather Moon, Ice Moon, Trees Broken Moon, Moon When the Little Lizard's Tail Freezes off Moon
- **February**: Snow Moon (snowy conditions), Hunger Moon (scarcity of food sources)
  Other names: Storm Moon, Trapper's Moon, Black Bear Moon, Elder Moon, Wind Moon, Exorcising Moon
- **March**: Worm Moon (earthworms come out at the end of winter)
  Other names: Storm Moon, Lenten Moon, Crow Moon, Chaste Moon, Wind Strong Moon, Big Clouds Moon, Earth Cracks Moon, All Leaf Split Moon
- **April**: Pink Moon (appearance of phlox flowers that bloom in early spring)
  Other names: Wind Moon, Planter's Moon, Deep Water Moon, Ashes Moon, Big Wind Moon, Moon on Grass Appearing, Sprouting Grass Moon
- **May**: Flower Moon (abundance of flowers)
  Other names: Mother's Moon, Hare Moon, Corn Planting Moon, Moon of the Shedding Ponies, Moon When Ice Goes Out of the Rivers
- **June**: Strawberry Moon (the time when strawberries are ripe)
  Other names: Strong Sun Moon, Honey Moon, Hot Moon, Moon When the Buffalo Bulls are Rutting, Corn Moon, Plant Moon, Turning Moon
- **July**: Buck Moon (when antlers appear on the male deer, stags)

Other names: Blessing Moon, Thunder Moon, Hay Moon, Mead Moon, Buffalo Rutting Moon, Rain Moon, Red Salmon Time Moon

- **August**: Sturgeon Moon (large number of fish appear in the lakes)
  Other names: Corn Moon, Dog's Day Moon, Wart Moon, Red Moon, Wheat Cut Moon, Autumn Moon, Grain Moon, Blackberry Patches Moon
- **September**: Harvest Moon (harvesting of crops)
  Other names: Dying Grass Moon, Barley Moon, Leaf Yellow Moon, All Ripe Moon, Corn in the Milk Moon, Big Feast Moon, Little Wind Moon
- **October**: Hunter's Moon (the hunting, slaughtering and preserving meats for use during the coming winter months)
  Other names: Blood Moon, Moon of the Changing Seasons, Deer Rutting Season Moon, Falling Leaves Time Moon, Basket Moon, Falling River Moon
- **November**: Beaver Moon (beavers become active preparing for the winter)
  Other names: Mourning Moon, Frosty Moon, Snow Moon, All Gathered Moon, Freezing Moon, Initiate Moon, Killing Deer Moon
- **December:** Cold Moon (winter has arrived)
  Other names: Long Nights Moon, Oak Moon, Moon of the Popping Trees, Ashes Fire Moon, Middle Winter Moon, Big Freezing Moon.

The Dakota Sioux appear to have been more descriptive in their moon names:

- **January:** Moon of the Terribles
- **February:** Moon of the Raccoon or the Moon When the Trees Pop

- **March:** Moon When Eyes are Sore from Bright Snow
- **April:** When Geese Return in Scattered Formation
- **May:** When Leaves are Green, or the Moon to Plant
- **June:** When Berries are Ripe
- **July:** Moon of the Summer
- **August:** Moon When All Things Ripen
- **September:** Moon When the Calves Grow Hair
- **October:** Moon When Quilling and Beading is Done
- **November:** Moon When Horns are Broken Off
- **December:** The Twelfth Moon.

According to the Celts of Ireland, as well as other people residing in the British Isles, the moon was referred to by names that reflected what was happening in the environment around them:

January: Quiet Moon
February: Moon of Ice
March: Moon of Winds
April: Growing Moon
May: Bright Moon
June: Moon of Horses

July: Moon of Claiming
August: Dispute Moon
September: Singing Moon
October: Harvest Moon
November: Dark Moon
December: Cold Moon

In 725 CE, English monk Venerable Bede set about recording some of the Anglo-Saxon names that were being used:

January: Wolf Moon
February: Storm Moon
March: Chaste Moon
April: Seed Moon
May: Hare Moon
June: Dyad Moon

July: Mead Moon
August: Corn Moon
September: Barley Moon
October: Blood Moon
November: Snow Moon
December: Oak Moon

Other countries around the world also have names for specific moons. The Chinese, for example, record the moons as follows:

January: Holiday Moon　　**July**: Hungry Ghost Moon
February: Budding Moon　　**August**: Harvest Moon
March: Sleepy Moon　　**September**: Chrysanthemum Moon
April: Peony Moon　　**October**: Kindly Moon
May: Dragon Moon　　**November**: White Moon
June: Lotus Moon　　**December**: Bitter Moon

For those of us living in the Southern Hemisphere, not all of these folk names may be appropriate for our moons, even if the names are moved six months around to reflect our seasonal differences. While this idea is commendable, it does not always reflect the uniqueness or vastness of the Australian landscape in particular. One example that I have observed on social media is the attempt to refer to the September full moon as 'Worm Moon', a name given to the March full moon by the Algonquian peoples of Canada. As mentioned previously, while March is the time when earthworm castings can be seen in North America after the winter, in most parts of Australia, September is already late spring, especially where I live, and therefore, such castings are not visible.

It is important to keep in mind that not every culture or group of Indigenous people had names for the full moons. While Australia has the longest continuous line of human habitation, the calendars of the Aboriginal peoples tend to be more seasonally based than lunar. As a result, no common group of moon names have been found. Another interesting point is that many groups saw the moon as a man who was pursed across the sky by a sun woman; the couple occasionally met during an eclipse.

The Yolngu people from north-eastern Arnhem Land in Australia's Northern Territory, for example, call the moon 'Ngalindi'. Originally, he was a fat lazy man (the full moon), for which he was punished by his wives, who chopped bits off him with their axes, producing the waning moon. He managed to escape by climbing a tall tree to follow the sun, but was mortally wounded, and died (the new moon). After remaining dead for three days, he rose again, growing round and fat (the waxing moon), until, after two weeks, his wives attacked him again. The cycle continued to repeat every month. Until Ngalindi first died, everyone on Earth was immortal, but he cursed humans and animals so that only he could return to life. For everyone else, death would thereafter be final.[43]

According to Associate Professor Duane Hamacher[44], in the Torres Strait (between the top of Cape York, Australia and Papua New Guinea), the moon plays an important role in the local culture, identity and daily life. The best time to fish is at a neap (low amplitude) tide that occurs during the first or last quarter because the water is clearer and the fish do not move as fast.

One Meriam Elder from the Murray Islands, Uncle Segar Passi, teaches that during the dry season ('Sager') the cusps point upwards, making the moon resemble a bowl used to collect water. Cumulus clouds appear in the sky and the water is choppy. When the moon tilts to its side and the seas are calm and mirror flat, this is because the water pours out of the bowl and falls like the rain during the wet season ('Kuki').

Across the Tasman Sea, the Māori of New Zealand brought their Polynesian mythology with them from their original homeland, the mythical land of Hawaiki. One name in particular is Marama, a word used throughout Polynesia meaning 'moon' or 'light'. In the Cook Islands, Marama was a lunar god who fell in love with and married Ina, the goddess of light. To the Māori, Marama was seen as a moon goddess and the sister of Ra, the sun. Just after the middle of each lunar month, Marama becomes seized with disease and thus wanes. Her sickness consumes her as she gradually disappears from sight. When she becomes excessively weak, she bathes in the Living Water of Tāne (the god of the forests and bird). These waters heal her; Marama gradually has her light and strength restored.

It is also interesting to note that the Māori also assigned a specific name for each night of the moon. This was because the moon guided the people in what foods they could or could not eat, when certain plants were ready to plant or crops were ready to be harvested, as well as when certain rituals and other observances were to be undertaken, much like the Torres Strait Islanders, as mentioned previously.

A way around this lack of information for appropriate moon names, regardless of where you live, is to make your own. Indeed, this is something that I suggest to my students. For example, I associate the March full moon with the grape harvest that is taking place in the surrounding wine-growing areas, although this activity sometimes commences earlier or even later depending on the ripeness of the grapes. August usually marks the time that the almond trees begin to flower around the small town of Willunga, located south of Adelaide. The wattle trees are also in flower at this time. Another observance is that, while not a native of Australia, the jacaranda trees with their delicate pale lilac flowers are very noticeable in November. A number of jacaranda-lined streets around Adelaide are truly beautiful to wander down when these trees are in full flower. The breeding cycles of particularly native or migrating animals can also be added to these flora observations.

Taking my own advice on board, the following are some examples of moon names that I tend to use because they reflect what is happening where I live in South Australia:

- **January**: 'The Moon of the Red Earth', because at this time of the year, here in South Australia the countryside is dusty, dry and red as it is in the height of summer.
- **February**: 'Anticipation Moon', as we wait for the return of the cooler days and longer nights. I also refer to the February full moon as 'Bushfire Moon' because this month often heralds the hottest temperatures, and therefore, many areas around where I live are on high

bushfire alert. 'Full Red Moon' is another appropriate name because the moon often has a reddish tinge to it due to the haze of the scorching summer heat.

- **March**: 'Moon of the Vine' or 'Harvest Moon', which reflects the grape harvest that is taking place in the surrounding local grape-growing areas, in particular the Barossa Valley, the Adelaide Hills, the Clare region and McLaren Vale.

- **April**: 'Moon of the Returning Green', as the autumn rains begin to fall after the harshness of summer, encouraging the land to become green once more. In many parts of Australia, the apple harvest is underway, so 'Apple Moon' could be another name.

- **May**: 'Whale Moon', because this marks the start of the migration undertaken by the southern right whales from Antarctica to the warmer waters of Encounter Bay, south of Adelaide, as well as other places around coastal Australia. This migration continues until the end of August, so any of these subsequent months could also be called 'Whale Moon'. In other parts of the country, the first of the frosts arrive, so 'First Frost Moon' could also be used.

- **June**: 'Moon of the Winter Rains'. June is traditionally the wettest month in South Australia. With the winter solstice occurring in June, 'The Long Night's Moon' could be a suitable alternative because at this time of the year, the moon has its highest trajectory in the sky and the sun has its lowest. Another name with a more Australian flavour could be 'Dingo Pup Moon' because June marks the end of the dingo breeding cycle and when the first litters begin to appear.

- **July**: 'Moon of the Courting Cuttlefish', which occurs in the waters around Whyalla, South Australia, as they migrate en masse to mate and lay eggs.

- **August**: 'Wattle Moon' marks when the Golden Wattle (*Acacia Pycnantha*) is apparently flowering throughout South Australia, from late winter and early spring onwards. Other names could be 'Kangaroo Moon' or 'Wallaby Moon' because this is the time of the year when joeys begin to emerge from their mothers' pouches and explore their environment.
- **September**: 'Moon of the Swooping Terror', because the breeding season for the Australian magpie commences and these birds are known to swoop unassuming pedestrians. In northern Australia, the second part of September and the first part of October is often the best time to fish for barramundi, so 'Barramundi Moon' could be used. Closer to home, my wisteria climber is in full flower and as the evenings warm, I love sitting outside with its delicate scent on the breeze.
- **October**: 'Honeybee Moon', which reflects that since spring is now in full swing in South Australia, the honeybees are working hard pollinating plants and gathering the nectar that they turn into honey. Another name could be 'Waking Moon' because the flora and fauna appear to be rather active and extremely noticeable, especially after the winter months.
- **November**: 'Harvest Moon', which marks the time when harvesting of the wheat crops commences in South Australia. An alternative moon name for November could be 'Rose Moon' because the roses begin to flower, especially within my garden.
- **December**: 'Moon of Festivities' reflects that as the end of the calendar year approaches, people are transitioning into the festive mood with lots of parties and merriment to be had. An alternative name for the December moon could be 'Abundance Moon' because this is the time that my vegetable garden shows its bounty. A further

alternative name could be 'Strawberry Moon' or even 'Summer Fruits Moon' because these fruits are in abundance at this time of the year.

Making regular observances of what is happening in your own local environment will not only enable you to develop a deeper connection with the land (referred to as *dadirri*, a word taken from the Ngan'gikurunggurr and Ngen'giwumirri languages of the Daly River Aboriginal people, who live south of Darwin that means 'deep listening'), but will also enable you to formulate a list of names for the moon that is more appropriate to where you live regardless of the hemisphere. This certainly helps here in Australia because of the vastness of this continent as a whole, not to mention the number of small microclimates. This means that it is almost impossible to find a 'one size fits all' approach when it comes to discovering appropriate names to suit the moon, just like when it comes to working with the seasonal wheel of the year.

Gods and Goddesses of the Moon

Ancient cultures considered the sun and moon divine symbols, and therefore, attributed genders to them. Today, we are probably more familiar with the moon being associated with feminine, a goddess, whereas the sun is considered more masculine, a god. Such gender association is considered to date back to the ancient Greek culture. Prior to that time, the ancient Babylonian people recorded their moon god, Sin, as first in the spiritual world, whereas in Hindu mythology, the moon god, Chandra, rode across the sky in a silver chariot that was pulled by deer. Further, as I mentioned in the previous section, within Aboriginal traditions, the moon is often seen as male whereas the sun is viewed as female.

The following is a collection of lunar deities known throughout the ancient world:

- **Arianhrod**: Welsh goddess who appeared in the Fourth Branch of *The Mabinogi* (a collection of Welsh myths). She was the daughter of Don, an originating Mother Goddess and the sister of two magicians, Gwydion and Gilfaethwy. While not a lunar goddess as such, Arianhrod's palace, Caer Arianhrod, is used as the Welsh version for the constellation Corona Borealis.

- **Artemis**: Considered the original personification of the moon, who was known to both the Greeks and the legendary Amazons. Worshippers paid homage to her on nights of the full moon by revelling in the forest under the moon's light. She was associated with the waxing moon in more modern times.

- **Auchimalgen**: A Chilean lunar goddess who cared for and watched out for the human race. She protected humankind from evil spirits. Legend says she turns red when an important person is about to die.

- **Bendis**: The moon goddess and wife of the sun god Sabazius, who was worshipped with orgiastic rites. Thracians made her popular in Attica, and in 430 BCE her cult became a state ceremonial in Athens, with torch races at the Piraeus.

- **Chandra** (also Chandraprabha): Hindu Lord of the Moon who was born after his mother was swallowed by the moon. Chandra is often shown with multiple heads, or holding a hare, which is sacred to him. He was the ancestor of the Chandra-vansa, the lunar race, from which Krishna, the eighth avatar (incarnation) of the god Vishnu, was descended. Chandra was associated with soma, the magical drink of the gods. His female counterpart was Candi, and the two were said to take turns – one month the moon would be Candi; the next it would be Chandra.

- **Chang-O**: Chinese moon goddess. According to legend,

she was the wife of a famous archer to whom the gods had promised immortality. Chang-O stole and drank her husband's magical potion, and therefore, she was forced to escape his wrath by fleeing to the moon in the shape of a frog. She is represented in the dark spots of the moon as a three-legged frog.

- **Cybele:** Originally a Phrygian goddess, Cybele is considered a very ancient goddess whose worship in Anatolia is believed to predate the Bronze Age. An image of Cybele depicts her seated on a throne with one hand resting on the neck of a lion while the other holds a circular frame drum or tambourine (tympanon), which was said to evoke the full moon because it was covered with the hide of the sacred lunar bull.

- **Dae-Soon:** Korean moon god who, along with his sister Hae-Soon, climbed a tall tree when they were chased by a tiger. When the tiger came to climb a tall tree, the children prayed to the gods to save them. An iron chain descended from the skies, which enable the children to arrive in the Land of the Gods away from the tiger. Here, Dae-Soon was transformed into the moon and his sister transformed into the sun.

- **Diana:** Roman assimilation of the Greek moon goddess, Artemis. Diana was often portrayed riding the moon, with a bow in her hands. She was frequently worshipped out in the open so she could look down at her faithful.

- **God D:** Mayan god of the moon and night sky, referred to in ancient manuscripts, but given no name. Numerous Mayan 'letter gods', as the nameless are called, have been assigned letters by scholar Paul Schell. God D was portrayed as an old man with sunken cheeks, wearing a serpent headdress. He was sometimes identified with Kukulcán, God of Mighty Speech, or Itzamna, sky god and Mayan culture hero.

- **Hekate**: Greek moon goddess who came out at night carrying a torch and accompanied by hounds. She was said to frequent crossroads, where statues to her were erected. A Triple Goddess, she was sometimes pictured as having the heads of a dog, a horse and a serpent. Worshippers paid tribute on nights of the full moon by leaving offerings at her statues. As Queen of the Night, Hekate ruled spirits, ghosts and infernal creatures such as ghouls. She was the patroness of witchcraft.

- **Hina**: Polynesian moon goddess. In Hawaiian mythology, her full name was Hina-hanaia-I-ka-malama, which means 'the woman who worked in the moon'. Various stories mention how she went there. In one story, she sailed her canoe to the moon. In another, her brother, angered by noise Hina was making after a night of heavy drinking, threw her into the heavens. In Tahitian and Hawaiian myths, she grew weary of beating out tapa and escaped her drudgery by fleeing to the moon. In another Hawaiian myth, a chief lured her up from a land under the seas, and from Hina's gourd originated the moon and the stars.

- **Ishtar**: Babylonian goddess who ruled the moon, derived in part from the Sumerian goddess, Inanna. In some accounts, Ishtar was the daughter of the moon god Sin and sister of Shamash, the sun god. According to legend, on a trip to the Underworld to find Tammuz, her dead lover, she had to shed her clothes, which caused the moon to darken. On her return trip, as she regained her clothes, the moon brightened again.

- **Ix Chel**: Mayan goddess of the moon. Ix Chel and the sun were lovers, but because the sun was always jealous, it was a stormy relationship. The sun would routinely tell her to leave heaven, only to set off to find her again. Travelling the night sky, Ix Chel would make herself invisible whenever the sun approached.

- **Juno:** Roman sky and moon goddess. The appearance of a new moon would bring out her women worshippers.
- **Khonsu:** Egyptian moon god, the son of Amun, god of the air and Mut, a Mother Goddess. Khonsu, whose name means 'he-who-traverses-(the-sky)', is depicted as a mummified youth holding a crook, a flail and a sceptre. On his head were representations of crescent and full moons. As a lunar god, he helped Thoth to reckon time. Because of his influence, women conceived and multiplied their young. Khonsu was also an important god of healing and is said to have healed Ptolemy IV of serious illness. Khonsu's principal temple was at Thebes.
- **Luna:** To the Romans, Luna was the divine embodiment or personification of the moon as a goddess. She was worshipped particularly at the new and full moons.
- **Mama Quilla:** Incan moon goddess who protected married women. Her most famous temple was erected at Cuzco, seat of the Inca Empire. She was portrayed as a silver disc with feminine features. It was said eclipses resulted when Mama Quilla was eaten by a heavenly jaguar.
- **Marama:** A lunar god from the Cook Islands who fell in love with and married Ina, the goddess of light. However, to the Māori, Marama was a moon goddess and the sister of Ra, the sun.
- **Nanna:** Sumerian moon god who was the first born son of Enlil and Ninlil, brother of Utu-Shamash (the sun god) and in some interpretations Inanna/Ishtar (goddess of love and sexuality). Earlier version to the Assyrian god Sin.
- **Selene:** A Greek goddess of the full moon who was the daughter of Hyperion and Theia, and sister of Helios (the sun) and Eos (the dawn). She was wooed and won by

Zeus and by Pan. She also fell in love with a shepherd prince, Endymion, and visited him nightly while he slept. (Zeus granted the mortal Endymion immortality on the condition that he remained eternally asleep.) Wearing wings and a crescent crown, Selene rode in a chariot pulled by two white horses.

- **Sin**: Moon god worshipped by the Assyrians, Babylonians and Sumerians. Sin was the son of Enlil, the storm god; his principal place of worship was at Ur. According to some myths, he begot Shamash the sun god, Ishtar, who ruled the moon and planet Venus, and Nusku, god of fire. Sin was personified as a turbaned old man with a long beard the colour of lapis lazuli. Every night, he rode in her barque, a brilliant crescent moon, across the sky. The moon was his weapon, and he was the enemy of all evil doers who lurked about at night. Sin also was a god of wisdom and advised other gods. Mount Sinai may have been originally dedicated to him.

- **Soma**: The Vedic (Hindu) god of the moon and of soma juice, the nectar of the gods. Soma was also Lord of the Stars, Plants and Brahmans. He married 27 or 33 daughters of Daksha and neglected all but one, causing Daksha to curse him to die of consumption. As he weakened, so did all things below on Earth. Daksha mitigated the curse to a monthly waxing and waning. Soma begot a lunar race of kings. The soma drink, a narcotic, believed to have divine powers, was offered in rites to the gods and was drunk by the Aryans. Later, only the three highest castes were permitted to drink soma, and then in religious rites only.

- **Thoth**: A lunar god of the Egyptians, worshipped in the form of an ibis, Thoth's origins are obscure. One myth says he was the son of Horus, springing from the forehead of Seth, who was impregnated by swallowing

Horus's seed on a lettuce leaf. An important deity, Thoth had numerous functions. He was god of timekeeping and was often depicted wearing a crescent moon on his head. He invented writing and was scribe and messenger to the gods. He recorded the judgement of the dead. He was the heart and tongue of the sun god Ra. Most importantly, he was the god of wisdom and magic, and ruled everything concerning the arts and sciences. Thoth authored 42 books containing all the wisdom in the world; they later became known as the Hermetica. The Greeks identified Thoth with their own god, Hermes; from these two deities came the mythical figure Hermes Trismegistus, or 'thrice-great Hermes'.

- **Yellow Woman**: Huntress goddess of the Keres, a Pueblo tribe. Yellow Woman is similar to the Roman Diana and also appears to have lunar associations; her name itself is evocative of moonlight. She appears in certain myths that explain the various moon phases and why the moon can sometimes be seen during the day. In one particular myth, Yellow Woman is killed at night. Her brother, Arrow Youth, searches for her with the help of Great Star. When he states that he wants his sister to be alive during the day, Arrow Youth is told by the chief of spirits that Yellow Woman will stay away for four days. Impatient, he begins to search for her among melon rinds, which are symbols of the crescent moon. Arrow Youth first finds her heart and then her head, which he washes. Yellow Woman finally puts on a dress and is seen during the day.
- **Yemoja**: Ocean Goddess of Brazilian Macumba. Yemoja is often depicted as a mermaid and is therefore associated with the moon, water and feminine mysteries. She is seen as the protector of women, and governs everything pertaining to women; particularly the birth and bearing

of children. According to myth, when Yemoja's waters broke, it caused a great flood, creating rivers and streams, and the first mortal humans were created from her womb.

Within contemporary witchcraft and a number of other modern pagan spiritual traditions, the moon is often associated with the Triple Goddess, comprising the Maiden (the waxing moon), the Mother (the full moon) and the Crone (the waning or dark moon). This connection of the goddess with the moon stems back to a work by Robert Graves[45] as opposed to having any actual historical association. Graves himself was possibly influenced by the work of British classical scholar Jane Ellen Harrison.[46] I have discussed this concept in great detail in my earlier books, *In Her Sacred Name: Writings on the Divine Feminine* and *Contemporary Witchcraft: Foundational Practices for a Magical Life*; it is also fairly widely documented on the internet, so I will not delve into any more detail here.

Lunar Symbols

A number of specific symbols are associated with the moon. The following is a list of things that have lunar connections that you can incorporate into your lunar rituals and spell workings:

- **Ambrosia**: The feminine mysteries of the menstrual cycle – the re-creative power of menstrual blood. Called soma among the Hindus, red claret of the faeries, and wise blood.
- **Bat**: A nocturnal creature that symbolises rebirth as it emerges from womb-like caves at dark only to return prior to dawn.
- **Blood**: Red has always been considered the colour of life and is the colour of the mother aspect of the Triple Goddess (Maiden, Mother and Crone), indicative of her fruitfulness through menstruation and birth. Altars and

people were consecrated by being sprinkled with blood in ancient times. Today, this is done with salted water.

- **Boat**: The moon was called the 'Boat of Light' by the Babylonians. Egyptians depicted the crescent moon with the horns turned upward either as part of the lunar deity's headdress or carved sky-boats, such as the ones pictured in the temple of Isis.

- **Bull, cow**: Originally the lunar symbol of the Great Mother with the horns representing the crescent moon, the bull later came to represent the sun gods. However, it was often still connected with a moon goddess, such as Cybele or Attis. The cow is the feminine symbol of both the moon and Earth. Egyptian goddesses connected with the cow include Isis, Hathor and Neith.

- **Cat**: To the Egyptians especially, the cat was a moon creature, and sacred to such goddesses as Isis, Bast, Artemis, Diana and Freyja. When Diana became known as queen of witches in the Middle Ages, the cat was associated with witchcraft and goddess worship.

- **Circle**: The circle was symbolic of the moon long before it was attributed as such by the sun gods. In Scotland, the Orkney Islands are still called 'Temples of the Moon'. The ancient Greek divinatory tool known as 'Hekate's Circle' was a gold sphere with a sapphire in its centre, and was hung on a thong of ox hide.

- **Crow, raven**: This bird was frequently associated with the dark moon goddesses, in particular the Irish battle queen, the Morrigan, owing to its black colour. The Morrigan also took on the guise of a raven or crow in her battle aspect.

- **Dew, rain**: Many cultures associate these forms of condensation with the moon. The early dew after a full moon is said to heal and improve beauty if rubbed into the skin. Certain phases and signs of the moon are purported to be conducive to rain.

- **Dogs**: Canines have long been associated with moon deities, especially crescent new moon mightiest of all dog-wolf supernatural beings, according to a Norse story. Packs of hunting hounds, such as the Alani of Diana, represent the dangerous energies of the moon.
- **Fish**: Some cultures symbolised the moon with a fish instead of a snake. Some moon goddesses were depicted with fishtails, akin to mermaids.
- **Frog**: A traditional lunar symbol. Sometimes called a toad, Hekat the frog goddess was connected with birth in ancient Egypt.
- **Groves**: Groves of trees were often sacred to the moon mother, especially if they held springs, pools or lakes. Ceremonies of drawing water and pouring it were part of her rituals. If a grove contained a grotto where water came directly out of a rock, it was especially sacred.
- **Hare, rabbit**: Many cultures around the world, including those of Tibet, China, Africa, Ceylon, and some Native Americans, said that a hare lived on the moon along with the ruling moon deity: especially associated with lunar goddesses.
- **Horns**: Bull or cow horns have always been connected with the moon and moon deities. Cattle, water buffalo and bison horns have been recovered that have 13 notches carved into them; the Goddess of Laussel is an example (as mentioned previously). These notches represent the 13 moon months of a seasonal year. The Greek Hera was also called *Keroessa* ('Horned One') in her aspect of Io, the moon cow.
- **Labrys, double Axe**: A goddess and moon symbol, said to have been one of the weapons preferred by the Amazons. A thunderbolt was said to have been given in this shape to the Amazons by Hera. In Crete and at Delphi, the

labrys was a ceremonial sceptre.

- **Lamp**: The moon is called by many the lamp of the night. The close connection with the moon's light is demonstrated by the additional titles attached to goddess names such as Juno Lucina and Diana Lucifera.

- **Mirror**: The moon is called the 'heavenly mirror' in Central Asia and many other parts of the world. The mirror is a goddess symbol, sometimes called a soul-carrier or soul-catcher. Some cultures believed that the souls of the dead went to the moon to await reincarnation.

- **Moth**: It is suggested that moths use the moon as a primary reference point and have the ability to calibrate their flight paths because Earth's rotation causes the moon to move across the sky.

- **Owl**: A night hunter possessing large eyes, the owl has long been associated with the moon. Considered the ruler of the night and seer of souls, the Egyptians considered the owl a symbol of death, night and cold. To the Greeks, however, it was an emblem of wisdom and the goddess Athena. Its staring eyes connected it with Lilith, Minerva, Blodeuwedd, Anath and Mari. The owl has long been associated with the moon, wisdom, sacred lunar mysteries and initiations.

- **Scythe, sickle:** A symbol of the crescent moon that was used by the Amazons and women who worshipped moon goddesses, particularly older or Crone goddesses. Even the druids used a moon-shaped sickle for their sacred ceremonies.

- **Silver**: This metal has long been regarded as the moon's metal; silver was used for divinatory cups.

- **Snake**: As a goddess symbol, the snake is the same as the spiral when it is coiled. Each turn of the coil marks a day in the lunar calendar. Zigzag lines represent snakes. Serpents were associated with the dark moon because they were considered related to the Underworld. Some dark moon goddesses were depicted with snakes as hair. There are pictures showing Cybele offering a cup to a snake. In the mythology of Mexico are tales of the woman serpent (moon) who is devoured by the sun, a description of an eclipse or the phases of the moon.

- **Sow**: The white sow has been associated with moon deities from the Celtic lands to the Mediterranean. It was connected with Astarte, Cerridwen, Demeter, Freyja and the Buddhist Marici.

- **Spiral**: The spiral, whichever way it turned, represented an aspect of the Great Goddess and the moon. The upward and downward spiralling, or in and out, can be compared with the waxing and waning of the moon. The Greek Crane Dance, probably originally performed in Crete by the bull-dancers, was danced around a horned altar, which was part of the labyrinth. Spirals appear on some ancient goddess statues, primarily replacing what would be eyes.

- **Wheel**: Though the wheel has most often been a sun symbol, there were occasions when it represented the moon. The silver wheel belonging to the Welsh goddess Arianrhod is really the moon.

- **Willow**: A moon tree sacred to such dark moon goddesses as Hekate, Circe and Persephone, the willow (*helice*) gave its name to the Helicon, abode of the nine muses, the orgiastic abode of the moon goddess.

- **Wolf**: The wolf howls at the moon, as do dogs; they hunt and frolic by moonlight. The moon priestesses of many cultures were adept at astral travelling and shape shifting, both talents usually practised at night. They also practised rituals, dancing and singing, outdoors under the moon. A Roman festival, the Lupercalia, was in honour of the wolf goddess Lupa or Feronia. The Norse believed that the giant wolf Hati chased the moon, and in the final days, it would eat this celestial body.

- **Yin and yang**: This Chinese symbol represents the joined powers of the male and female, positive and negative; in other words, a cyclical alternation of duality. At one point in ancient Chinese history, this design symbolised the phases of the moon – the light and dark cycles. Much of the ancient world spoke of the two ladies or two mistresses of the moon.

Crystals and the Moon

Throughout history, many crystals and semi-precious stones have been especially associated with the moon. Moonstone, a feldspar crystal with a pearly white sheen, is said to contain the image of the moon. Ancient Romans believed moonstone was formed from solidified beams of moonlight and that their lunar goddess, Diana, could be seen within the crystal. This belief about the solidified moonbeams is also found in India, where a piece of moonstone was said to be set into the forehead of the moon god, Chandra, and would grow dimmer or become brighter with the waning and waxing of the moon. Chandra's full name, Chandra Shekara, means 'person who wears the moon'. Moonstone was given as a traditional wedding gift because it was considered a 'love stone' with the ability to reconcile estranged lovers.

Over time, moonstone has been used as a protection for all kinds of travellers and has been synonymous with the moon, magic, love, good fortune, enhancing psychic abilities and dream recall. During the Middle Ages, moonstone was used for scrying the future.

As a crystal of protection for women and children, especially pregnant women and babies, moonstone has a long rich history of being used to help with women's reproductive health – from easing menstrual problems to assisting a woman in childbirth. It has been used for centuries to enhance fertility, such as the ancient practice of women sewing moonstones into their clothing if they would like to have a child, which continues today for some Middle Eastern women. It is also believed that wearing a piece of moonstone jewellery during the full moon while making love increases fertility.

Due to its ability to help soothe wild hormones, moonstone makes a great gift for teenagers and women going through various changes in their life (pregnancy, menopause). Being the 'crystal of the goddess', moonstone can help sync up the rhythms of lunar energy to the rhythms of a woman's body. Even human-made crystals, such as opalite moonstone, contain properties similar to those of the real moonstone.

Medieval metaphysicians considered chalcedony the chosen crystal of the moon because it was the birthstone relating to Cancer (the crab), the sign of the zodiac ruled solely by the moon. A translucent quartz, chalcedony varies in colour from milky white to pale blue-grey or even warm tan. Considered able to cheer melancholy spirits, chalcedony was believed by the ancient Romans to protect against the evil eye, and Mediterranean seamen believed the crystal would protect them from drowning. European folk medicine claimed that a touch of chalcedony upon the brow would reduce fever, bring about tranquillity to a troubled mind and accelerate recovery.

Certain other crystals have a sympathetic resonance with the cool, subtle energies of the moon. These crystals can help align the wearer's vibrations with the moon, inducing clearer dreams, clairvoyant awakening, deeper perceptions and emotional understanding.

- **New to full moon crystals:** White, clear or watery bright-coloured crystals are used during these phases of the lunar cycle such as:

  - **Aquamarine:** An ideal dream crystal, helps with

tuning into the rhythms of the sea and the depths of one's own spirit.

- **Azurite:** Helps tune into the psychic world.
- **Celestite:** In its blue or white varieties, helps to link to spirit guides.
- **Clear quartz:** Has a strong affinity with the moon and can be used to enhance and direct the moon's rays in ceremonies of healing or invocation.
- **Moonstone:** Used to balance the hormonal cycle, calm any unsettled emotions, especially over parenting issues, and induce lucid dreaming.

Circular white stones can also be used to represent the full moon.

- **Waning to Dark Moon Crystals:** Black, dark or cloudy crystals are used during these phases of the lunar cycle such as:

  - **Black onyx:** Enhances clear focus, amplifies intentions, encourages sensibility and clear thinking, enhances protection, shields from negative energies and assists in grounding.
  - **Black tourmaline:** Promotes a healthy mood, helps to detox from heavy metals and environmental pollutants, supports a reduction of anxiety and stress, supports a healthy immune system, supports disengaging obsessive behaviours.
  - **Jet:** Calms all the subtle bodies, clears a heavy head and can help in lifting of depression. Especially useful for clearing negative inner or outer environments where the build-up of tension is preventing sleep.

Circular black or dark stones have also traditionally been associated with and used during the dark moon phase. Keep an eye out for them on the riverside or beach and carry them when you are feeling confused or disorientated.

Moon Prayer Beads

One way that I like to use crystals to connect with Lady Lunar is through the use of prayer or devotional beads. These beads are made in a similar way to the mala beads that are used in Hindu and Buddhist practices. The devotional moon beads that I make through my Etsy store consist of a combination of three times three (representing the Maiden, Mother and Crone concept as found within many goddess or Earth-centric spiritual paths) or 13 (the number of new or full moons in one year). However, you can use any pattern that appeals to you.

The crystals I use are Sri Lankan moonstone or opalite (human-made version of moonstone if I cannot obtain the authentic moonstone beads) for the waxing moon, red coral or red jasper for the full moon and black onyx for the waning moon. Again, you can use whatever crystals you are drawn to.

I then thread the appropriate number of crystal beads that I am using onto beading wire in the sequence that I have chosen. If I am making the 13-bead style set, I thread the 13 beads of each moonstone, red coral and black onyx onto the beading wire with each section separated by a silver spacer bail from which a moon charm is hung. Alternatively, I thread only three of each crystal (nine beads being a complete section) and separate them with a silver spacer bail and moon charm. To complete the devotional beads, I thread the wire through a larger silver pearl bead (guru or mountain bead) and finish with a combination of focal beads, a handmade tassel or a larger moon charm.

A further alternative is to hand knot each bead as in a traditional mala. If I am using this method, I do not always include the silver bail spacer beads.

Once completed, the Lunar Prayer or devotional beads can be used in a similar fashion to that of a mala, for which specific prayers or affirmations are chanted with each crystal or section of crystals. For example, you can use the moonstone or opalite crystal beads to draw something into your life, considering they are associated with the waxing moon; the red coral can be used for gratitude and the black onyx to release or remove things from your life.

Plants of the Moon

The moon has a face like the clock in the hall;
She shines on thieves on the garden wall,
On streets and fields and harbour quays,
And birdies asleep in the forks of the trees.
The squalling cat and the squeaking mouse,
The howling dog by the door of the house,
The bat that lies in bed at noon,
All love to be out by the light of the moon.
But all of the things that belong to the day
Cuddle to sleep to be out of her way;
And flowers and children close their eyes
Till up in the morning the sun shall arise.
('The Moon' by Robert Louis Stevenson)

Several herbs bear marked resemblances to the moon in her various phases, both in colour and shape of plant, fruit and flower. The white fruits of fennel grow in pairs of curved oblong shapes that seem to represent the waxing and waning lunar crescents. The lily – in particular the arum lily – long an associate of lunar goddesses, has round, bell-shaped flowers that are frequently bright white and bears oblong to crescent-shaped leaves. The fruit of the almond generally is also pure white and oblong to crescent shaped.

Magically speaking, herbs of the moon affect the subconscious mind. They are a very good aid in the development of intuition and psychic abilities as well as in remembering dreams. Because they have such a primary effect on the subconscious, they can be used to successfully influence it to break old habits and recall past lives.

Traditionally, the moon reigns over plants whose foliage is white or silver, or which have pale cream, yellow or bright white flowers. Other plants that the moon reigns over are those that flower during the night. These include anise, camphor, iris, jasmine, lily, poppy, violet, willow, lotus, moonwort, mugwort and sandalwood. Some flowers that are associated with the moon include anise, blue lotus, clary sage, ginger, hibiscus, milk thistle, poppy and rose. Vegetables that are also connected with the moon include cabbage, cucumber, lettuce and pumpkin.

- **Adder's Tongue** (*Ophioglossum vulgatum*): A fern found in damp meadows and shaded woodlands. Its leaves have healing virtues and are most effective when gathered during the waning moon. A single leaf imparts insight to its bearer.
- **Camphor** (*Cinnamomum camphora*): An evergreen tree, native to China and Japan, with aromatic wood and leaves producing a pungent substance widely used in medicine.
- **Clary** (*Salvia sclarea*): This garden herb's name is a contraction of 'clear eye', referring to the use of its seeds to heal eye irritations.
- **Gardenia** (*Gardenia jasminoides*): A native of China, its exquisite white flowers and lovely scent define it as a lunar emblem.
- **Jasmine** (*Jasminum officinale*): A night-blooming plant of tiny white flowers in the shape of stars with unforgettable fragrance.
- **Lemon** (*Citrus limonia*): The fruit of the lemon tree provides the ultimate in cooling beverages. Lemons are used in witchcraft to counter ill-wishing and as guard-charms.

- **Lily** (*Lilium candidum*): The Madonna Lily has been cultivated for over a thousand years. Its pure white trumpet-shaped flowers bloom in late summer to greet the sign of Cancer and the rulership of the moon.

- **Moonwort** (*Botrychium lunaria*): An uncommon variety of fern found in dry meadows and hillsides. Its crescent-shaped segments in pairs along the frond are like tiny moons and give the plant its names. Renowned for healing fresh wounds and according to folklore, moonwort opens locks and unshoes horses that trod upon it.

- **Mugwort** (*Artemisia vulgaris*): The 18th century Swedish botanist Linnaeus chose Artemisia as the genus name for silvery and grey-green leafy herbs. Mugwort was sacred to the moon goddess in ancient Greece, where it provided protection from evil and preserved energy on a journey.

- **Poppy** (*Papaver somniferum*): The opium poppy is native to Greece and Asia. Although its narcotic properties can ease pain, fear of addiction precludes its use. Every source, ancient to modern, lists the poppy as a moon plant.

- **Southernwood** (*Artemisia abrotanum*): A herb praised by Greek and Romans for its magical qualities as a love charm. A strong and strangely pleasing scent comes from its leaves.

- **Trefoil** (*Trifolium pratense*): The perennial red clover, one of the sacred Celtic herbs, was held in high esteem by Druids, who saw it as a symbol of Earth, sea and sky.

- **Willow** (*Salix alba* and *nigra*): The white and black (pussy) willow trees have long been associated with water and the moon.

- **Wormwood** (*Artemisia absinthium*): Classical myths recount that the Greek goddess of the moon presented this aromatic herb to Chiron, the Centaur who taught the healing arts to Greek heroes.

You can use these plants of the moon as offerings during your rituals, or make appropriate oils and incenses from them, as is mentioned in the earlier section. It is important to remember that the properties of some plants can change, so it is crucial that you undertake your research, especially if you want to make an incense that will be burned.

Wands made from willow are considered a sacred ritual tool for lunar workings. I was gifted such a wand a number of years ago and I use it solely during my moon rites.

Part V
Lunar Miscellaneous

O Trivia, Goddess, leave these low abodes,
And traverse o'er the wide ethereal roads,
Celestial Queen, put on thy robes of light,
Now Cynthia named, fair regent of the night.
At sight of thee the villain sheaths his sword,
No scales the wall, to steal the wealthy hoard.
O may thy silver lamp from heaven's high bower
Direct my footsteps in the midnight hour!
('Trivia' by John Gay)

Lunar Miscellaneous

Lunar Relationships

In Part III, I discussed how the astrological sign the moon is in at the time of your birth (known as the birth or natal moon) can have an impact on your life. In this section, I will briefly explain how our birth moons can influence our relationships with other people. Of course, when it comes to astrology, it is best to consider the placement of all planets in your natal chart. However, the following can be used as a guide.

Fire Moon Signs: Aries, Leo and Sagittarius

People who have their birth moon in a fire sign tend to be passionate, direct, forthright and full of energy. They say what they mean and are extremely open and honest, even if they tend to lack a degree of subtlety. In relationships, they come across as being highly sexed and passionate but can be volatile as well. They also like being the centre of attention. Two fire signs together can result in a highly charged and extremely passionate relationship but one that may quickly burn out. A more favourable relationship would be when joined with an air sign because these two moons tend to inspire each other. If joined with a water sign, this relationship could be intense and sexually exciting or end up with the parties at odds with each other. Fire and earth moon signs tend to be the most difficult combination because each party will struggle with managing the other's emotions.

Water Signs: Cancer, Scorpio and Pisces

People with their birth moon in a water sign tend to be emotional, highly intuitive and very creative. Their emotions are extremely visible; they are known to wear their hearts on their sleeves, as well as being easily moved to tears. This is because the moon is in its natural element, water. As mentioned previously, when teamed up with a fire sign, this relationship can commence as being very sexually exciting; however, over time, water does tend to extinguish flames. Two water moons together could feel like being adrift in a sea of romance and sentimentality where neither party has a true connection with reality. A relationship with an air moon partner may feel comfortable and romantic; however, things could become tough when there is a need to deal with the ups and downs of reality. Water and earth moon signs tend to be the most compatible.

Air Signs: Gemini, Libra and Aquarius

People who have their birth moon in an air sign tend to be intellectual and talkative. They are always communicating through one means or the other, yet not necessarily baring their souls. This is because air signs can be seen as being emotionally aloof and even somewhat hesitant in exploring the deeper realms of their emotions. Despite this, air and water moons are often seen as being very compatible despite being at either end of the emotional spectrum. When coupled with a fire sign, as mentioned previously, this relationship can be very strong because fire relies on air to thrive. Conversely, a partner with an earth moon may weigh down the light and expansive emotions of an air moon. Finally, when two air moons are together this relationship will be filled with communication, rather lively and a lot of fun, yet may miss the vital spark of passion.

Earth Signs: Taurus, Virgo, Capricorn

People who have their birth moon in an earth sign tend to bring emotional stability to any partnership. They tend to be rather cautious, patient, calm and kind. Earth moons are not known for outward displays of emotion, yet they are extremely sensual, loving and faithful. Relationships that are ideal for earth moons are those that last the distance. Two earth moons together are strong but not all that exciting. Yet both partners will endure things without any thrills and excitement. A better match for an earth moon is with water. This is because both partners are able to balance out the other person's emotional nature. Earth and air moon relationships can be somewhat strained because neither party truly understands the other's way of relating and dealing with the world. However, they are often able to reach a mutual understanding. As mentioned previously, earth and fire moons tend to find it extremely difficult to understand and deal with each other's emotions.

Essay: Moon Worship in the Modern Age

The following essay originally appeared in *A Mantle of Stars: A Devotional Anthology to the Queen of Heaven*[47] and has been slightly adapted for inclusion in this publication.

I stood silently gazing upward at the evening sky. Mist was creeping over the ground, and the hum of the traffic could be heard in the distance, but only if I focused on it. The clouds had built up all afternoon, threatening to rain but despite the ground arching up, desperate for some relief, like Geb arching up to the Sky Goddess Nut in ancient Egyptian papyri, nothing fell. A slight breeze played with the candle flames. I wondered whether the same breeze would be enough to move the clouds, to expose Her, the moon, the heavenly queen who rules the night sky. Deep down inside, I knew the answer – it was the same every month.

As I gazed upward, I started humming to myself. Totally unaware at first, but then my lips began to move as if the words of the chant were forcing themselves out:

Moon, sister moon, shining so high
Smile down upon me, full face in the sky.
Moon, sister moon, with your silver glow
Whisper your secrets, tell me what you know.[48]

Softly at first there was just my lone voice, but soon other voices joined in as the lines were repeated over and over again.

All eyes were focused skyward, arms were raised as we called to the moon to show her regal self tonight. Shine on us, beautiful Lady. Show us your brilliance this evening. Depart the clouded veils and bless us with your presence.

Suddenly a gasp was heard. There was a break in the clouds, and we were bathed in spectacular lunar light for the first time that evening. I smiled to myself and bowed my head in respect. She has never let me down since I started holding these open gatherings in a local park of over a decade now.

Our voices returned to a gentle hum as we faced inwards and held hands. Each person visualised the lunar light entering the top of the head, which is represented by the crown chakra, or the Qabalistic Kether. This energy was slowly drawn down to the chest area, the heart chakra, where it was met with energy that has also been drawn up on Earth. Here, at the centre the Qabalists refer to as Tiphareth (the Golden Sun) the two energies mingled, the cosmic and the *terra firma*, before we visualised sending it around the circle through our right hands, and receiving it through our left hands. This is deosil, sun wise, in the Southern Hemisphere. As each of us visualised receiving and releasing the energy, we also connected with the next person in the circle.

I started up another chant – "The circle is cast around about, a world within and a world without. The circle is cast around about" – encouraging attendees to join in. The chanting grew louder. The visualisation grew stronger with the voices until everything peaked. There was silence for a moment. A few glances darted around the circle from those who had not attended a gathering before. These were greeted by the reassuring smile on the faces of the rest of us. Yes, the circle was cast and with a faint drift of mist across the park, we were really between the worlds.

We then faced each quarter in turn, commencing with east and moving in a sunwise direction around the circle, as the elemental quarters are acknowledged. The wind picked up for a moment as if acknowledging each call before dropping again.

We faced east again as I called to the Queen of the Midnight Skies, who had disappeared momentarily behind a cloud:

By your ancient names we call to thee
Diana, Ishtar, Artemis, Ixchel, Isis, Selene, Astarte, Selene
O Queen of Heaven, Queen of the Earth
Mother of all Mysteries
We give praise to you this night
You who are the most radiant in all the heavens
The starry night sky is your body
That stretches out above us, embracing us, comforting us
We adore you, O Ruler of the midnight skies
As you ebb and flow silently through our lives
Weaving your dreams and enchanting us with your mysteries
Descend tonight and join us, O gracious Lady of the Night
Descend tonight and join us as we honour you.
As we praise you, she who we adore.
Ea, Binah, Ge.

The last line was slowly vibrated over and over again. The others around me joined in, arms extended upward again, eyes now open and gazing upward. Come to us, come to us. We stood in anticipation, waiting for her to acknowledge our call. We did not have to wait too long before we were again graced with the presence of the Queen of Heaven as her lunar light danced.

From the centre of the circle, I retrieved a bowl of fresh rainwater to which I had added a few drops of essential oil I had made especially for the night – a mixture of jasmine and frankincense. While it was a simple bowl made out of cut glass, it glittered and shone in the moonlight as I offered it up to the goddess. Walking around the circle, I anointed all those who were in attendance. Once done, participants were invited to make themselves comfortable on the ground, where they were guided into a lunar pathworking whereby a lunar bridge connected each person in turn with an aspect of the goddess pertinent to them at this current time. For this to occur, the stresses and connections of daily life needed to be put to the side:

I tell the participants: "Breathe in slowly and deeply, breathing in the moonlight. As you breathe out, exhale, feel your body relax. Open your crown chakra, visualise the silvery moonbeams entering the top of your head. Then slowly move down your body with each breath that you take, before exiting from your base chakra into the earth. As the moonbeams move down through your body, they take with them all tension, stress, and anxiety you may be feeling and drains these into the earth, where they become cleansed and recycled into energy, ready to be used again.

"Let the purifying light flow into you. Let the healing light flow through you. Let the nurturing light cleanse and heal you."

I waited a few moments, visualising what I had just said since I also needed cleansing and healing from trying to keep up with the demands of modern living. Our awareness was then brought back to the moon in the sky above us and the moonbeams reaching out to us. These beams were now forming a bridge, a connection between us and the Queen of the Midnight Skies. In our minds, we journeyed across this bridge to meet the aspect of the goddess whose message and guidance was most relevant to us at this particular time. Then the words came:

I am the ancient Mother who watches over you
I have been worshipped since humankind first gazed upwards
My temples reside only within your heart
That is where I can always be found
Call to me – I will come
Pray to me – I will hear
Ask of me – I will always provide.

My messages arrive on the gentle wings of a butterfly
For I am the soft breeze on your face
And I am also the tornado that shakes your world.
You see me in the first spring flower and the last harvested fruit
I am the weed in the footpath and I am the most delicate orchid.
Call to me when you are weary
For I will be your strength.
Think of me when you feel alone
For I always walk beside you.
You are my sacred child – free yourself and come to me.

Each breath that we took strengthened the connection we individually felt with the particular aspect of the goddess. Each breath that we took relaxed us further, assisting in the separation between the mundane everyday world and that other realm where magic and psychic thought ruled. Each breath that we took enabled our inner self to be free from its physical constraints.

After a while I felt a soft hum emerging as yet another chant was forcing itself out between my lips. The hum was bringing people back to the here and now. Because we had been touched by the goddess, it seemed appropriate that we sing to her:

We all come from the goddess, and to her we shall return
Like a drop of rain, flowing to the ocean.[49]

Smiles began to appear on the faces around the circle. The dampness from the grass started to enter our consciousness. It was time to stand; it was time to move. We rose to our feet, some uneasy at first, hands reached out for the others around the circle, and all the while, the singing continued. Stepping to the right, we moved in the deosil direction for the Southern Hemisphere with our feet following the 'grapevine' step. The chant changed to the 'Goddess Chant'.[50] The pace quickened as the energy began to rise. Sensing it had reached its peak, I directed it to be sent wherever it was needed the most.

Some participants wanted to share their experiences of the pathworking while others stayed in silent contemplation, as if trying to make sense of it all. The penny will drop, I assured them, maybe not now, maybe not tomorrow or even next week – but it will make sense.

With a degree of reluctance, we began to open the circle. We thanked the goddess for her presence and guidance, as well as the elemental forces for their contribution. For those who had never attended a group ritual before, some appeared to be slightly overwhelmed by the experience and needed a bit of extra grounding. I smiled to myself – the simplicity of things could be so meaningful to others. Will I see them again next month? Who knows? Some people return; others do not. One thing I was certain of was that everyone who attended tonight would be spending a bit more time gazing at the night sky.

Lunar Places of Power

Around the world, there are a number of specific sites that were built in alignment as specific lunar observations. Earlier in this book, I mentioned how the stone complex of Callanish on the Isle of Lewis, Scotland, was built in alignment with the lunar standstill. The ancient Mayans of Central America were also thought to have purpose built an astronomical observatory in their city of Chichén Itzá, on Mexico's Yucatán Peninsula, which has been voted as one of the new Seven Wonders of the World.

During the classical period of Mesoamerica (250–900 CE), the Mayans were believed to have had detailed mathematical knowledge of the appearances and movements of the moon, which they considered an important lunar deity. They were able to make accurate predictions of celestial events, linking them with the role of their lunar and other celestial deities. At the height of their power, the Mayans produced codices in the form of folder illustrated books containing detailed calendars and almanacs that included imagery of lunar gods and accurate astronomical tables that included patterns of lunar cycles and the timing of eclipses. The most famous surviving document is the Dresden Codex written in the 11th or 12th century as a copy of an original that was produced three or four centuries earlier.

Today, at Chichén Itzá (whose name has been translated to mean 'at the mouth of the well of the Itzá people'), while not lunar orientated, the Kukulcán Pyramid was built so that at each spring equinox the shadow of the setting sun would cast a shadow of a serpent writhing down the steps of the pyramid.

Located some 37 km north of Mexico's capital, the colossal pyramid temple structure at Teotihuacan can be found. This site is believed to have been built to the moon and the sun, and the Great Square of the Moon was almost certainly an important religious centre for centuries. The Pyramid of the Moon is believed to have been completed around 250 CE and excavations near the base of its pyramid staircase uncovered a tomb containing a male skeleton and items made from obsidian and green stone.

A platform on top of the pyramid was used to conduct ceremonies in honour of the Great Goddess of Teotihuacan, known as the Teotihuacan Spider Woman, who was a goddess of water, fertility and Earth, as well as all creation itself. Opposite the altar is a plaza, sometimes referred to as the 'Plaza of the Moon', that consists of a central altar and an original construction with internal divisions, comprising four rectangular and diagonal bodies that formed what is known as the 'Teotihuacan Cross'.

On the other side of the world, on the Mediterranean island of Sicily, the remains of an ancient Greek temple can be found that was originally built facing the setting full moon near the winter solstice. Known as the temple of Demeter and Persephone, the shrine forms part of a collection of temples that once stood in full glory in Akragas, later known as Agrigento. The so-called

'Valley of the Temples' is believed to be some 2,500 years old and it was a native of Akragas, Greek philosopher Empedocles (490 to 430 BCE), who first divided matter into the four elements that we know today (earth, air, fire and water), and who also observed that the moon shone with light reflected from the sun. This temple of Demeter and Persephone seems to be rather unique in that it is preceded by a fountain sanctuary where votive deposits have been found, including a statuette of Persephone. One of the two altars contains a central well that contained the remains of offerings, while at the back of the temple is an esplanade area that would have offered a clear view of the full moon over the hill of the acropolis.

Today in the Valley of the Temples, the remains of sacred sites dedicated to Heracles, Olympic Zeus, Demeter and Persephone, Juno, Concordia, Vulcan and Aesculapius can be found, a number of which have specific nocturnal alignments to the heavens.

The Man in the Moon

The man in the moon came down too soon
And asked the way to Norwich
He went by the south and burnt his mouth
With eating hot pease porridge.
(Author unknown)

There has been a long-standing European belief that there is a man in the moon and how he arrived there was often through some wrongdoing here on Earth. In *Inferno*, the first part of Dante's *The Divine Comedy* (published in 1321), this man was Cain, the surviving son of Adam and Eve, who was punished to forever circle the earth after killing his brother Abel:

For now doth Cain with fork of thorns confine
On either hemisphere, touching the wave

Beneath the towers of Seville. Yesternight
The moon was round.[51]

However, it was not all doom and gloom, as a traditional ballad that was sung at the court in Holywell stated that the Man in the Moon spent his time drinking claret:

Our man in the moon drinks clarret,
With powder-beef, turnep, and carret.
If he doth so, why should not you
Drink until the sky looks blew?

In the 19th century, RA Procter produced a collection of moon related myths entitled *Myths and Marvels of Astronomy*[52] in which was recorded the story of an elderly man collecting sticks or chopping wood on a Sunday. On his way home with his bundle of wood, he met a rather handsome man dressed in a suit walking towards the local church. The suit-wearing man stopped and asked the elderly stick collector, 'Do you know that this is Sunday on Earth when all must rest from their labours?' The stick collector responded by laughing and saying, 'Sunday on Earth or Monday in heaven, it's all one to me'. According to the story, the stranger retorted, 'Then bear your bundle forever, and as you value not Sunday on Earth, yours shall be a perpetual moon day in heaven; you shall stand for eternity in the moon, a warning to all Sabbath-breakers', before vanishing. The elderly man found himself, together with his collection of wood, on the moon, where he stands today.

This story may have originated from a biblical tale since in Numbers XV 32–36, a man is found gathering sticks on the Sabbath day and is brought before Moses and Aaron. No one is certain what to do with the man until Yahweh tells Moses that the man must die and that the whole assembly must stone him outside the camp. Therefore, the man is killed.

When WHJ Bleed observed the Bushman people of Africa,

he noted that contained within their astrologically orientated mythology, the moon was looked upon as a man who incurred the wrath of the sun, and is consequently pierced by the knife (the rays) of the latter. This process is repeated until almost the whole of the moon is cut away and only a little piece is left, which the moon piteously implores the sun to spare his (the moon's) children. From this little piece, the moon gradually grows again until it becomes a full moon, when the sun's stabbing and cutting processes recommence.[53]

Even John Jamieson noted that the moon was viewed as being of 'the masculine gender in respect of the earth, whose husband he was supposed to be; but as a female in relation to the sun, as being his spouse'.[54]

I cannot help but wonder whether the change in gender reference to female was a result of science and acknowledgements at the time discovering the moon's inferiority to the sun. Prior to this, the moon was considered superior to the sun and was referred to as being male.

The Rabbit in the Moon

In the Far East, a rabbit is said to reside in the moon. Believed to have originated in China before spreading through other Asian cultures, the rabbit is a companion of the moon goddess, Chang'O, who is constantly pounding the 'elixir of life' for her or making rice cakes. These cakes contain only four ingredients – golden syrup, lye water, vegetable oil and plain flour – which are all mixed together into a dough, which is then filled with lotus paste before being baked.

Within Buddhism, stories can be found of a monkey, an otter, a jackal and a rabbit who are all resolved to practise charity on the day of the full moon as a way of demonstrating great virtue. When they come across an old man begging for food, the monkey gathers fruits from the trees, the otter collects fish from a river, and the jackal finds a lizard and a pot of milk-curd. The rabbit, however, only knows how to gather grass, so it decides to offer its whole body by throwing itself into a fire that the old man has prepared. The rabbit does not burn, which puzzles all the animals until the old man reveals that he is actually Sakra, the Lord of the Devas and ruler of heaven. Humbled by the virtue of the rabbit, Sakra draws the likeness of the rabbit on the moon for all to see.

Aliens and the Moon

It has long been believed that the moon was home for aliens. In the 1820s, Bavarian astronomer Franz von Paula Gruithuisen claimed to have viewed cities containing sophisticated buildings, roads and forts on the moon through his telescope. He called these alleged inhabitants 'lunarians', and despite his assertions being laughed at by his colleagues, a small crater on the moon was named after him.

Von Paula Gruithuisen was not alone in his thoughts. Around the same time, prominent British astronomer and composer Sir William Herschel (1738–1822), known for discovering two moons of Saturn (Mimas and Enceladus) as well as Uranus with his sister Caroline, also believed that aliens lived on the moon. In 1835 the *New York Sun* published a series of articles, known as the 'Great Moon Hoax', that incorrectly credited Herschel's son John, a famous astronomer in his own right, with such a discovery that described these 'moon men' as being furry and winged, and the women resembling bats. Sir Herschel is said to have remained convinced of his claims until his death in 1822.[55]

Lunar Weather Lore

If, at her birth, or within the first few days, the lower horn of the moon appears obscure, dark or in any way discoloured, there will be foul and stormy weather before the full.

If the moon is discoloured in the middle of its body, the weather will be stormy about the full.

If the upper horns are thus affected, storms will come around the wane.

If the moon has a halo, rain and wind or snow and wind are coming. The bigger the halo, the nearer the rain or snow.

If the moon outshines the halo, bad weather will not come.

The open side of the halo tells the quarter from which the wind or rain may be expected.

A Lunar Ritual

For this ritual, you will need a bowl containing some salt (sea) water and a large shell, nine smaller seashells, three tealight candles and incense (such as jasmine, frankincense or ylang that is attributed to the moon).

Before you commence the ritual, you will need to create a chant that expresses your desire.

The altar is placed facing the western quarter (associated with water) and should be round if possible. In the centre, place a bowl of salt water, with a white seashell in the centre of the bowl. While doing this, whisper the name of the goddess who rules the current phase of the moon, under which you are working. For example, the new moon belongs to the Maiden Goddess, such as Diana or Artemis. The full moon is associated with the Mother Goddess, such as Cybele or Selene. The waning moon belongs to the Crone or Underworld Goddesses, such as Hekate (in her Underworld aspect).

Around the bowl, set nine white shells, forming a crescent (horns upward, as in a smile). If the magic is for the gain of something, place the shells from right to left. If the magic is for the removal or loss of something, place the shells from left to right. As each shell is placed, chant the name of the goddess who presides over the goal of the magical influence you desire.

Matters concerning beginnings and manifestations are ruled by the Maiden Goddess. Matters involving 'forces', energies or powers are under the influence of the Mother Goddess. Matters of death, decline and stagnation are ruled by the Crone.

Place three tealight candles in a triangle around the bowl. If you want to manifest something on the physical plane, construct a reversed triangle, with the top of the triangle pointing towards you. If you want to manifest something on the astral plane, construct an upright triangle, with the top pointing away.

During the magical work, the energy is focused into the altar bowl, to 'enchant' the salt water. Begin by passing your right hand, palm down, over the bowl in a deosil[56] direction. Perform nine passes, then do the same with your left hand. You will need to create a chant that describes your intent. As you chant, blow gently upon the water slightly disturbing the surface. Formulate the incantation to be as descriptive as you can, about what you desire. For example, if you are wishing to manifest love in your life using the new moon:

Virgin Huntress, shining bright
Spear my lover on this night
As you grow so does our love
On earth above and move above.

Once you have spoken the incantation into the bowl, it is time to release the 'charge'. There are a number of techniques to do this. The first is to boil the water and observe the steam as it evaporates. Continue to boil it until all of the water is gone. As the steam rises up, repeat your incantation and watch the steam as it moves upward. It is carrying off your magic, so that it may take effect. Think about your desire as you watch it.

Another method is to pour out the contents of the bowl into the sea or ocean. You can also pour the water onto the ground, but if you choose to do this, take care to further dilute the water first because salt can damage the pH in the soil. As you dispose of the water, recite a simple rhyme spell, such as:

Water to Water
A witch's spell,
I give this stream
To speed it well.

Exercise: Receiving the Moon's Energy

The following techniques can be used to receive the energy of the full moon. All you need is a mirror or a bowl of water in which the reflection of the moon can be observed. You may also like to make yourself up a blend of anointing oil such as the recipe provided with respect to the full moon in Part I of this book. Alternatively, mix up to 10 drops of jasmine, sandalwood or camphor essential oil into 10 ml of a suitable carrier oil such as jojoba or even olive oil. To strengthen your connection, you may wish to wear white colouring or go 'sky clad' (wearing nothing at all).

Position yourself and your reflective surface where you can see the moon in your mirror or bowl of water. For women or anyone who strongly identifies as female, anoint your sacral chakra (just below the navel) with the full moon oil in an upward pointing crescent shape. If you are a man or identify as male or non-binary, then anoint your solar plexus (just above the navel) with the oil.

As the scent of the oil begins to fill the air, deepen your breathing into your diaphragm while keeping your focus on the image of the moon within your reflective surface. With each breath that you take, visualise that the light of the moon captured in your mirror or bowl of water is being reflected into you through your third eye, the ajna chakra, which is located in the middle of your forehead.

As you continue to breathe, you may find yourself starting to go into a light trance. This is perfectly fine. Focus on your breathing and allow yourself to be 'moon blessed'. You may also like to vocalise the following short chant (which has been taken from a line of a declaration the Goddess made in Dion Fortune's novel *The Sea Priestess*[57] after being invoked) a number of times to add to your lunar experience:

Ea, Binah Ge.[58]

When you are ready to come back to normal consciousness, bring your awareness to your physical body, wriggling your fingers and toes. Take a few more deep breaths into your diaphragm and open your eyes. Remember to record your experiences in your journal.

A Goddess Full Moon Ritual

This ritual first appeared in my previous book about the goddess, *In Her Sacred Name: Writings on the Goddess*. I have included it here because it contains information that may be of benefit if you have never performed any kind of ritual before.

A beginner can experience a great deal of hesitancy when it comes to performing rituals, the biggest fear being 'What if I do something wrong?' Most of the time, the Goddess, whatever aspect you wish to call upon, will simply be delighted that you are wishing to acknowledge her, and should she wish to be honoured in a specific way, she will let you know.

A good rule of thumb to remember when working with any deity is to treat them as you would a special guest. Ensure that your clothes are clean (if possible, you may wish to acquire a special set of clothes or even a robe to wear when you are performing rituals). Should you wish to ask for something, ensure that this is done with respect; should you wish to offer something, ensure that it is the best that you can afford.

Most importantly do not forget to show your gratitude and say 'thank you'. There will be times when what we ask for and what we receive may be entirely different things. In such instances, it is still considered polite to show our gratitude.

If possible, perform this ritual outside under the light of the full moon. If this is not possible, try to position yourself so that you can view the moon (or at least a picture of the moon). While the following ritual has been written for a solitary practitioner, it can be easily adapted for a small group of friends.

Preparation

On the altar, in addition to any normal altar candles, have a candelabra (preferably silver) that holds three candles: white for the Maiden Goddess, red for the Mother and black for the Crone. If this is not available, then three separate white candles can be used, or a silver or purple coloured candle is also more than appropriate.

Have a chalice (silver or clear glass) containing a libation of wine or juice. You will also need to have a plate containing a biscuit or biscuits and a libation bowl into which some wine or juice and at least one biscuit will be placed as an offering.

The incense you use during this ritual should be lunar orientated (either specifically blended for the full moon or jasmine). You can use a cone or a joss stick, or granulated incense. If you use granulated incense, you will also need a charcoal brick. Jasmine, frankincense and sandalwood are scents often associated with the moon or general incenses. If you use joss sticks, then Indian 'temple' sticks such as Nag Champa are also rather pleasant to use. For people who are sensitive to aromatics, you may prefer to use essential oils or opt for no fragrance at all.

You will also need your tarot or oracle cards, or any other form of divination device if you wish to understand any divination.

Light the charcoal discs and add a pinch or two of resin-based incense on the charcoal disc or light the incense stick or cone as well as the altar candles. Say:

On this night of the full moon,
I celebrate the ancient mysteries that have been celebrated
By all those who have gone before me.

May the powers of the Goddess bless me on this night.
So mote it be.

Cast the circle using your wand or extended finger on your dominant hand, saying:

I cast this circle thrice about
To keep unwanted powers out
Three times three, do I go
Once for the Maiden pure as snow
Once for the Mother full and round
And once for the Crone barren bound.
By the power of three times three
In the name of the Goddess, so mote it be.

If you wish the call upon the powers of the four elemental powers, then the placement of these elements will depend on whether you live in the Northern Hemisphere or the Southern Hemisphere. If you live in the Northern Hemisphere, after you have used a compass to determine where the elemental directions are, begin by facing the east and say:

I call on air to lend me your powers of thought and inspiration.
Face the south and say:
I call on fire to lend me your powers of passion and determination.
Face the west and say:
I call on water to lend me your powers of emotion and compassion.
Face the north and say:
I call on earth to lend me your powers of grounding and foundation.

If you live in the Southern Hemisphere,[59] however, begin by facing the east and say:

I call on air to lend me your powers of thought and inspiration.

Face the north and say:
I call on fire to lend me your powers of passion and determination.
Face the west and say:
I call on water to lend me your powers of emotion and compassion.
Face the south and say:
I call on earth to lend me your powers of grounding and foundation.

Light the candles in the candelabra, starting with the white candle for the Maiden. Say each line as you light the corresponding candle:

On this night of the full moon, I come here to honour thee, sacred Maiden.
On this night of the full moon, I come here to honour thee, sacred Mother.
On this night of the Full moon, I come here to honour thee, sacred Crone.

When you have finished lighting the candles, stand before the altar and continue:

On this night of the full moon, I honour thee, Goddess, in your triple ways
White for the Maiden who is pure as snow
Red for the Mother, the creatrix of all life
Black for the Crone, whose knowledge is deep within.
I honour thee, Goddess,
You who was, who is and who shall always be.
So mote it be.

You may wish to 'sing down the moon'. One suitable song for this is *Moon Sister Moon* that can be found on the *Moving Breath* album and on YouTube at http://www.youtube.com/watch?v=4SCyrg8K0YQ:

Moon, Sister Moon, shining so high
Smile down upon me, full face in the sky.
Moon, Sister Moon, with your silver glow
Whisper your secrets, tell me what you know.

Continue with the song until you feel the presence of the Goddess. This 'feeling' may take a while. I find being able to see the moon helps during this. Alternatively, visualise the silver orb above your head with moonbeams streaming your body through your crown chakra. The beams then move through your body, pushing all toxins, anxieties and stresses through the soles of your feet into the earth where they will be purified.

You can now recite the 'Charge of the Goddess'[60] or any other piece of writing that will help you connect with the Goddess. The following (which has been adapted from the 'Charge of the Goddess') is where the goddess speaks to her worshippers:

Whenever you are in need of anything
Call to me and I will come to thee
I am the Goddess of the three moons.
I am mistress of the darkness night.
I am the richness of the green earth.
I am all that was, that is and that ever shall be.
I am the mistress of all mysteries and the keeper of all keys.
I am Queen of all living things, the Goddess of nature.
and the radiance of the moon.
Upon the richness of the earth, you will find my temples
Under the boundlessness of the sky you will learn my secrets
For my mysteries are those for all to be discovered.
Look for me and I will be found,
For within your soul I reside.
I am the most gracious Goddess who has been with you from the
beginning
And I shall be with you at the end of all desire.

Now is the time to undertake any divination work or meditate on any problem to which you are seeking an answer. When you are finished, pick up the chalice of wine (or juice) and while holding it upwards towards the moon, state:

I bless this wine (juice) in the name of the Maiden, the Mother, and Crone.
As I drink from this chalice, I drink from the womb of the Goddess
And in doing so, I partake in the mysteries of her
She who is Queen of All.

Pour some of the wine (juice) into the libation bowl before taking a few sips yourself. As you drink, savour the taste and contemplate the words that you have just said. Return the chalice to the altar. Take the plate of biscuits and holding it upwards, state:

I bless this cake in the name of the Maiden, the Mother, and Crone.
As I eat from this plate, I eat from the body of the Goddess
And in doing so, I partake in all the mysteries of her
She who is Queen of All.

Break off a piece of the biscuit and put it in the libation bowl, before eating the rest. As you eat, contemplate the words that you have just said.

Take a few moments to relax and draw in the energy of the ritual. If you are outside, spend time gazing at the moon, visualising her subtle energies dancing down the moonbeams to you.

When you are ready to finish your ritual, snuff out the Triple Goddess candles, using a candle snuffer or the back of a teaspoon, in reverse order, starting with the black candle, and say:

Ancient Crone, whose face is hidden from the starlit night, I thank you.
Bountiful Mother, nurturer of all and the giver of life, I thank you.

Maiden of wonder, the bringer of new ideas and inspiration, I thank you.

Say farewell to the four elements (if you have called them). These are farewelled in a manner similar to the way they were called into your sacred space. If you live in the Northern Hemisphere, face the east and say:

I thank you air for lending me your powers of thought and inspiration.
Face the north and say:
I thank you fire for lending me your powers of passion and determination.
Face the west and say:
I thank you water for lending me your powers of emotion and compassion.
Face the south and say:
I thank you earth for lending me your powers of grounding and foundation.

If you live in the Southern Hemisphere, then say farewell to the elements in this sequence, starting in the east:

I thank you air for lending me your powers of thought and inspiration.
Face the south and say:
I thank you fire for lending me your powers of passion and determination.
Face the west and say:
I thank you water for lending me your powers of emotion and compassion.
Face the north and say:
I thank you earth for lending me your powers of grounding and foundation.

Taking a final deep breath, and then call back your circle by stating:

I call back my circle and return this sacred space to this current time and place
May the spirit of the Goddess be forever in my heart.
Merry meet, merry part, and merry meet again.

Finally, snuff out the altar candles, and dispose of the contents in your libation bowl outside. If you live in a high-rise apartment, maybe dispose of the offerings on a grassed area that is not conspicuous.

The candles that you use for your full moon ritual should be kept and used only for this event. That way they can be imbued with the energy of the full moon.

Lunar Cakes

Lunar rites, especially those that take place within contemporary witchcraft, often include the sharing of cakes, or more appropriately biscuits, among the participants, but also with the chosen lunar deity. Here, they are left out in the open as an offering. The act of eating something after a ritual helps to ground you back into normal consciousness.

The following recipes can make up to four biscuits that can be used as offerings during moon-orientated rites. When stored in an airtight container, they can last for a couple of weeks. To make these moon biscuits you will need:

- 125 gm margarine
- 50 gm to 75 gm demerara sugar
- 3 drops vanilla essence
- 125 gm plain uncooked oatmeal
- 125 gm wholemeal flour
- Milk to moisten

Mix margarine to smooth, adding sugar and vanilla essence. Blend in oats and flour gradually moistening slightly with enough milk to make dough.

Roll to 5 mm thickness and cut into required crescent moon shapes before baking in a preheated oven at 180°C (350°F) for 12–15 minutes.

Almond Crescent Biscuits

- 1 cup butter
- ¾ cup sugar
- 1 pinch salt (if you are using unsalted butter, add ¼ tsp salt)
- ¾ cup finely chopped fresh almonds
- 2–2½ cups all-purpose flour

Begin by preheating the oven to 180°C (350°F). While the oven is being heated, in a large bowl beat butter until light and fluffy, add sugar and beat again until fluffy. Scrape down the sides of the bowl and add almond, salt and flour (add 2 cups to begin with and add 1 tablespoon at a time, up to 8 tablespoons if needed). Beat until all ingredients are combined.

Bring dough together with your fingers and the break off small pieces. Shape into crescent moon shapes, and place on ungreased baking paper. Bake for approximately 15 minutes. While the biscuits are still warm, roll them in icing sugar. Alternatively, allow the biscuits to cool completely and then lightly dust with icing sugar.

An alternative recipe is:

- 1 cup grated almonds
- 1¼ cups all-purpose flour
- ¼ cup confectioners' sugar

- 1 egg yolk
- 1 whole egg
- ¼ tsp salt
- ¼ tsp cinnamon
- 4 tbsp unsalted butter, softened

Preheat the oven to 160°C (320°F) and line a baking tray with baking paper or non-stick spray.

Combine almonds, flour, salt, cinnamon and sugar. Mix well before adding butter, egg yolk and whole egg. Blend well and take dough ball out of bowl and place on plastic wrap or wax paper, cover and let chill in fridge for about 20 minutes.

Once chilled, take tablespoon-size pieces of dough and roll in your hand, making a long log, with the middle bigger and the ends smaller. Bend each log into a crescent moon shape.

Bake in preheated oven for 20 minutes. Let cool completely before dusting the tops of the biscuit with confectioners' sugar.

Lady Lunar, Midnight Queen
Who rules over the tides unseen
Your shining radiance across the sky
Bless me with your silver light
Queen of Heaven, Queen of the Stars
My love resides deep within my heart
I give thanks to thee, Lady Moon
For your blessings and your boon
Lady Lunar, Midnight Queen
Depart in peace until we meet again.

Resources

Internet Sites

- Astro Style: https://astrostyle.com/cosmic-calculators/moon-phase
- Astrodienst: https://www.astro.com
- Astronomical Society of Australia: https://asa.astronomy.org.au
- Astronomical Society of South Australia: https://www.assa.org.au
- Australian Indigenous Astronomy: www.aboriginalastronomy.com.au
- Free natal chart: Astrodiest.com
- Information on the different types of eclipses: https://www.space.com/15584-solar-eclipses.html
- Maramataka: The Māori Moon Calendar: https://researcharchive.lincoln.ac.nz/handle/10182/155
- Moon Calendar: Lunaf: www.lunaf.com/lunar-calendar
- NASA: The Danjon Eclipse Scale: https://eclipse.gsfc.nasa.gov/OH/Danjon.html
- Phases of the Moon: Astro-Seek: www.mooncalendar.astro-seek.com
- Royal Astronomical Society of New Zealand: https://rasnz.org.nz/in-the-sky/lunar-phases
- Timing of moon phases: Time and Date: www.timeanddate.com

Some of my Favourite Astrological Sites

- Astrobutterfly: https://astrobutterfly.com
- Astrology King: https://astrologyking.com
- Café Astrology: https://cafeastrology.com

- Forever Conscious: https://foreverconscious.com
- Molly McCord: https://www.youtube.com/c/MollyMcCordAstrology
- Pippastrology: https://www.pippastrology.com

About the Author

Frances Billinghurst has been a student of metaphysics, Goddess spirituality and the occult arts for most of her adult life. An initiate of a traditional style of contemporary witchcraft who founded the Temple of the Dark Moon in 1999, Frances is also a practising occultist, budding mythologist and esoteric lecturer. In 2003, Frances led the opening ritual of the New Zealand Pagan Fest with Chief Druid Philip Carr-Gomm, and in 2010, she was accompanied by occult philosopher Ramsay Dukes. She has also presented lectures at the Australia Wiccan Conference and the Australian Goddess Conference, worked with renowned Wiccan elders Janet Farrar and Gavin Bone, and held the position of secretary for the Pagan Alliance Incorporated (South Australia) for six consecutive years.

Aside from running an active coven, Frances is the author of *Contemporary Witchcraft: Foundational Practices for a Magical Life*, *Encountering the Dark Goddess: A Journey into the Shadow Realms*, *Dancing the Sacred Wheel: A Journey through the Southern Sabbats* and *In Her Sacred Name: Writings about the Divine Feminine*, and editor of *Call of the God: An Anthology Exploring the Divine Masculine within Modern Paganism*. A prolific writer, Frances has had articles appear in over 20 publications, including the Llewellyn *Witch's Calendar*, *The Cauldron* and *Circle*, as well as being a regular columnist for Australia's No. 1 spiritual lifestyle magazine, *Insight*, for 10 years. Her essays and poetry can also be found in numerous anthologies, including *Unto Herself: A Devotional Anthology for Independent Goddess* (edited by Ashley Horne and Bibliotheca Alexandrina), *The Faerie Queens* (edited by Sorita d'Este and David Rankine), *Queen of Olympos: A Devotional Anthology to Hera and Iuno* (edited by Lykeia and Bibliotheca Alexandrina), *A Mantle of Stars: A Devotional Anthology to the Queen of Heaven* (edited by Jen Connelly and Bibliotheca

Alexandrina), and *Blood, Bone and Blade: A Tribute to the Morrigan* (edited by Nicole Ross and Bibliotheca Alexandrina).

When she is not attempting to turn her patch of parched Australian dirt into something that slightly resembles the Hanging Gardens of Babylon, Frances also crafts an assortment of beaded jewellery and crystal mala beads, as well as devotional beads. These items are available for purchase through LunaNoire Creations at https://www.etsy.com/au/shop/LunaNoireCreations.

Endnotes

1. Charles Godfrey Leland, *Gypsy Sorcery and Fortune Telling: Illustrated by Incantations, Specimens of Medical Magic, Anecdotes and Tales* (Forgotten Books, 2008)
2. Ray, Amit, *Meditation: Insights and Inspirations* (Inner Light Publishers, 2015)
3. Gutzwiller, Martin C, *Moon-Earth-Sun: The Oldest Three-Body Problem* (retrieved from www.afhalifax.ca/bete/ DALEMBERTIMAGES/lune/ gutzwiller-moon-earth-sin%20rmp.70.589.pdf)
4. Neugebauer, O., *A History of Ancient Mathematical Astronomy: In Three Volumes* (Springer, 1975)
5. Moss, Robert, 'Plutarch in the Light of the Moon' (retrieved from http://mossdreams.blogspot.com/2018/01/ plutarch-in-light-of-moon.html)
6. Catholic Church apologises to Galileo (retrieved from http://www.baskent.edu.tr/~tkaracay/etudio/agora/ news/ Galileo.html)
7. Lunar Conception: A Discovery by Dr Jonas (retrieved from https://www.lunarium.co.uk/articles/jonas.jsp)
8. Shelley, Percy Bysshe, *The Complete Poems of Percy Bysshe Shelley* (Modern Library, 2000)
9. Rossetti, Christina Georgina, *Sing Song: A Nursery Rhyme Book* (Dover, 1968)
10. Naylor, Ernest, *Moonstruck: How Lunar Cycles Affect Life* (Oxford University Press, 2015)
11. Jackson, Kenneth Hurlstone, trans, *A Celtic Miscellany: Translations from the Celtic Literatures* (Penguin Books, 1971)
12. Boland, Yasmine, *Moonology: Working with the Magic of Lunar Cycles* (Hay House, 2016)
13. Emoto, Masaru, *The Hidden Messages in Water* (Atria, 2005)

14. Boland, Yasmine, *Moonology: Working with the Magic of Lunar Cycles* (Hay House, 2016)

15. Widdershins is a Scottish word (from the lowland Scots) meaning to move in a direction that is contrary to the sun's course, and that is considered unlucky. An alternative word is 'tuathal', from Scottish Gaelic. It is often described as moving in an anti-clockwise direction; however, for those of us living south of the equator, to move widdershins is to move in a clockwise direction. See my earlier book *Contemporary Witchcraft: Foundational Practices for a Magical Life* for a more in depth explanation.

16. Within contemporary witchcraft, our circles are usually cast in alignment with the sun, which rises in the east and sets in the west. In the Northern Hemisphere, the zenith, or peak of the sun throughout its journey is in the south, while in the Southern Hemisphere, this is the north. Therefore the 'dark quarter', where the sun never reaches, is the north if you reside in the Northern Hemisphere or the south in the Southern Hemisphere.

17. Deosil is a Scottish word meaning to move in a sunwise direction that is considered the 'prosperous course'. It is often described as moving in a clockwise direction. However, for those of us living south of the equator, to move deosil is to move in an anti-clockwise direction. See my earlier book *Contemporary Witchcraft: Foundational Practices for a Magical Life* for a more in-depth explanation.

18. This fragment was published by his wife, Mary Shelley, in either 1824 or 1839 (retrieved from http://www.poetryfoundation.org/poems/45115/art-thoy-pale-for-weariness)

19. Addison, Joseph, 'The Spacious Firmament on High' (retrieved from https://poets.org/poem/spacious-firmament-high)

20. Blue Moon (retrieved from https://en.wikipedia.org/wiki/

Blue_moon)

21. I write more about Lilith and her controversial role as a dark goddess in my book *Encountering the Dark Goddess: A Journey into the Shadow Realms* (Moon Books, 2021).

22. Macario, Marina, 'Black Moon Lilith' (retrieved from https://darkstarastrology.com /black-moon-lilith/)

23. Hamacher, Duane, 'The Moon plays an Important Role in Indigenous Culture' (retrieved from https://theconversation.com/the-moon-plays-an-important-role-in-indigenous-culture-and-helped-win-a-battle-over-sea-rights-119081)

24. Todd, Mable Loomis, *Total Eclipses of the Sun* (1894) (retrieved from https://earthsky.org/astronomy-essentials/whats-it-like-to-see-a-total-solar-eclipse)

25. Ibid.

26. Retrieved from http://www.daypoems.net/plainpoems/1020.html

27. Ogden, Daniel, Magic, *Witchcraft, and Ghosts in the Greek and Roman Worlds: A Sourcebook* (Oxford University Press, 2009)

28. Agrippa, Heinrich Cornelius, *Three Books of Occult Philosophy* (Llewellyn Worldwide Ltd, 1993)

29. Bell, Jessie Wicker, *The Witches Workbook: The Magic Grimoire of Lady Sheba* (Kensington Publishing Company, 1975)

30. Agrippa, Heinrich Cornelius, *Three Books of Occult Philosophy* (Llewellyn Worldwide Ltd, 1993)

31. Valiente, Doreen, *Witchcraft for Tomorrow* (Robert Hale, 1993)

32. Tully, Caroline, 'Drawing Down the Moon', Necropolis Now (retrieved from http://necropolisnow.blogspot.com.au /2009/03/drawing-down-moon.html)

33. Ogden, David, *Magic, Witchcraft and Ghosts in the Greek and Roman Worlds* (Oxford University Press, 2002)

34. Leland, Charles G, *Aradia, or the Gospel of the Witches* (retrieved from https://www.sacred-texts.com/pag/ aradia/ ara03.htm)
35. Hutton, Ronald, *The Triumph of the Moon* (Oxford University Press, 1999)
36. Adler, Margot, *Drawing Down the Moon: Witches, Druids, Goddess Worshippers and Other Pagans in America Today* (Penguin Books, 2006)
37. Pepper, Elizabeth, *Moon Lore* (The Witches' Almanac, 1997)
38. Original invocation written by the author.
39. Cunningham, Scott, *Complete Book of Oils, Incenses and Brews* (Llewellyn Publications, 2002)
40. When incense recipes call for 'parts', I personally equate this to the measuring instrument that I am using. For example, I have a specific spoon that I use when making my incenses. Therefore, when a recipe calls for '1 part', it equates to one spoonful, and likewise a '¼ part' is ¼ of the same spoon.
41. Agrippa, Henry Cornelius, *Three Books of Occult Philosophy* (Llewellyn Worldwide Ltd, 1993)
42. There is some debate around whether Algonquian is actually a language or a language group. This raises a degree of doubt over the authenticity of the moon names.
43. Australian Indigenous Astronomy (retrieved from www. aboriginalastrology.com.au)
44. Hamacher, Duane, 'The Moon Plays an Important Rule in Indigenous Culture' (retrieved from https:// theconversation.com/the-moon-plays-an-important-role-in-Indigenous-culture-and-helped-win-a-balttle-over-searights-1119081)
45. Graves, Robert, *The White Goddess: A Historical Grammar of Poetic Myth* (Faber & Faber, 1961)
46. Harrison, Jane Ellen, *Prolegomena to the Study of Greek Religion* (Cambridge University Press, 1902)

47. Connelly, Jen, ed, *A Mantle of Stars: A Devotional for the Queen of Heaven* (Createspace, 2013)
48. 'Moon Sister Moon' by Moving Breath, She Changes: A Collection of Songs from Healing Circles (Moving Breath, 1997)
49. Written by Zsuzsanna Budapest.
50. Written by Deena Metzger, this chant names seven goddesses: Isis, Astarte, Diana, Hekate, Demeter, Kali and Inanna.
51. Dante, *The Divine Comedy, Inferno,* canto 20, line 126 and 127. The Dante Dartmouth Project contained the original text and centuries of commentary.
52. Procter, R.A., *Myths and Marvels of Astronomy* (London, 1878)
53. Bleed, W.H.I., *A Brief Account of Bushman Folklore* (Juta, 1875)
54. Jamieson, James, *An Etymological Dictionary of the Scottish Language* (D.D. Pasley, 1880)
55. Simanek, Donald E., 'The Moon Hoax' (retrieved from https://www.lockhaven.edu/~dsimanek/hoaxes/moonhoax.htm)
56. Deosil means to move sunwise, which is to the left, or clockwise, in the Northern Hemisphere and to the right, or anticlockwise, in the Southern Hemisphere.
57. Fortune, Dion, *The Sea Priestess* (Red Wheel/Weiser, 2003)
58. Dion Fortune states that the Great Goddess is known by many names and is connected to three realms, space, Earth and water. Ea is older than time, the matric of matter and the root substance of all existence. Binah, the third sephira on the Qabalistic Tree of Life glyph, is known as the Supernal Mother, who gives form to the formless. Finally, Ge is the bringer of death, the receiver of the souls that have died before they are reborn again.
59. I go into more details about the differences between the

hemispheres in *Contemporary Witchcraft: Foundational Practices for a Magical Life* that include why there is a difference between elemental placements.

60. Originally written by Doreen Valiente.

Bibliography

Billinghurst, Frances, *Contemporary Witchcraft: Foundational Practices for a Magical Life* (Moon Books, 2021)

_____ *Dancing the Sacred Wheel: A Journey through the Southern Sabbats* (TDM Publishing, 2014)

Bollard, Yasmine, *Moonology* (Hay House, 2016)

Hamacher, D.W. and Norris, R.P., 'Eclipses in Australian Aboriginal Astronomy', *Journal of Astronomical History and Heritage Vol. 12* (2011)

Harley, Rev. Timothy, *Moon Lore* (2017)

Hulley, Charles E, *Dreamtime Moon: Aboriginal Myths of the Moon* (Reed Books, 1996)

Pepper, Elizabeth, *Moon Lore* (The Witches Almanac Ltd, 1997)

Index

MOON
BOOKS

PAGANISM & SHAMANISM

What is Paganism? A religion, a spirituality, an alternative belief system, nature worship? You can find support for all these definitions (and many more) in dictionaries, encyclopaedias, and text books of religion, but subscribe to any one and the truth will evade you. Above all Paganism is a creative pursuit, an encounter with reality, an exploration of meaning and an expression of the soul. Druids, Heathens, Wiccans and others, all contribute their insights and literary riches to the Pagan tradition. Moon Books invites you to begin or to deepen your own encounter, right here, right now.

If you have enjoyed this book, why not tell other readers by posting a review on your preferred book site.

Recent bestsellers from Moon Books are:

Journey to the Dark Goddess
How to Return to Your Soul
Jane Meredith
Discover the powerful secrets of the Dark Goddess and
transform your depression, grief and pain into healing
and integration.
Paperback: 978-1-84694-677-6 ebook: 978-1-78099-223-5

Shamanic Reiki
Expanded Ways of Working with Universal Life Force Energy
Llyn Roberts, Robert Levy
Shamanism and Reiki are each powerful ways of healing; together,
their power multiplies. *Shamanic Reiki* introduces techniques to
help healers and Reiki practitioners tap ancient healing wisdom.
Paperback: 978-1-84694-037-8 ebook: 978-1-84694-650-9

Pagan Portals – The Awen Alone
Walking the Path of the Solitary Druid
Joanna van der Hoeven
An introductory guide for the solitary Druid, *The Awen Alone* will
accompany you as you explore, and seek out your own place
within the natural world.
Paperback: 978-1-78279-547-6 ebook: 978-1-78279-546-9

A Kitchen Witch's World of Magical Herbs & Plants
Rachel Patterson
A journey into the magical world of herbs and plants, filled with
magical uses, folklore, history and practical magic. By popular
writer, blogger and kitchen witch, Tansy Firedragon.
Paperback: 978-1-78279-621-3 ebook: 978-1-78279-620-6

Medicine for the Soul
The Complete Book of Shamanic Healing
Ross Heaven
All you will ever need to know about shamanic healing and how to
become your own shaman...
Paperback: 978-1-78099-419-2 ebook: 978-1-78099-420-8

Shaman Pathways – The Druid Shaman
Exploring the Celtic Otherworld
Danu Forest
A practical guide to Celtic shamanism with exercises and
techniques as well as traditional lore for exploring the Celtic
Otherworld.
Paperback: 978-1-78099-615-8 ebook: 978-1-78099-616-5

Traditional Witchcraft for the Woods and Forests
A Witch's Guide to the Woodland with Guided Meditations and
Pathworking
Mélusine Draco
A Witch's guide to walking alone in the woods, with guided
meditations and pathworking.
Paperback: 978-1-84694-803-9 ebook: 978-1-84694-804-6

Wild Earth, Wild Soul
A Manual for an Ecstatic Culture
Bill Pfeiffer
Imagine a nature-based culture so alive and so connected,
spreading like wildfire. This book is the first flame...
Paperback: 978-1-78099-187-0 ebook: 978-1-78099-188-7

Naming the Goddess
Trevor Greenfield
Naming the Goddess is written by over eighty adherents and
scholars of Goddess and Goddess Spirituality.
Paperback: 978-1-78279-476-9 ebook: 978-1-78279-475-2

Shapeshifting into Higher Consciousness
Heal and Transform Yourself and Our World with Ancient
Shamanic and Modern Methods
Llyn Roberts
Ancient and modern methods that you can use every day to
transform yourself and make a positive difference in the world.
Paperback: 978-1-84694-843-5 ebook: 978-1-84694-844-2

Readers of ebooks can buy or view any of these bestsellers by
clicking on the live link in the title. Most titles are published in
paperback and as an ebook. Paperbacks are available in traditional
bookshops. Both print and ebook formats are available online.

Find more titles and sign up to our readers' newsletter at
http://www.johnhuntpublishing.com/paganism
Follow us on Facebook at https://www.facebook.com/MoonBooks
and Twitter at https://twitter.com/MoonBooksJHP